PAUL'S JOUI

ACTS 8-28

A 12-Week Mediterannean Cruise for Youth

By
Nancy Fisher

- ● **Twelve Exciting Lessons and Resources**

- ● **Take a "Mediterranean Cruise Adventure"**

- ● **Help students discover new life in Jesus Christ, see how Paul's life was changed, and tell the world the Good News**

- ● **Use with Paul's Journey: Then and Now Map**

What's Inside

R🌹SE
PUBLISHING

Introduction

The exciting 12 step-by-step lessons in this study guide for the map "Paul's Journeys: Then and Now" can be used in many creative ways by:

- **Sunday School classes**
  for a 12-week series or for supplements to lessons from Acts
- **Home Schoolers or Christian school classrooms**
- **Small groups**
- **Parents or grandparents**
  for Family Devotions or Family Night Activities
- **Vacation Bible School teachers** for curriculum
- **For a Children's Study** of Paul
  while parents are studying Acts in an Adult Bible Study

  Adaptable for individuals from children to adults.

  Sessions can also be divided to fit shorter time frames.

About the Author

Nancy loves to teach and see kids get excited about the Bible. She has taught Sunday School and VBS for 30+ years and is currently part of a sixth grade teaching team.

Nancy has written studies and devotions for family camps, youth camps, and retreats. She also enjoys theater and has written many short dramatic sketches as well as several full length stage productions. She uses her gifts as an artist and writer to stimulate her teaching.

Through drama, discussion, object lessons, crafts, activities, special guests, service projects, small groups, field trips and Bible study, Nancy and her team encourage their students to know and trust God. The air of adventure and exciting activities create a class and staff who can't wait to get to Sunday School each week.

Her love of teaching is matched by her passion for learning. Nancy returned to school when her older children reached their teens. She has earned an AA and BA and is currently working towards a Master's degree. Nancy and her husband live in Southern California. They have four grown children.

Nancy Fisher's Sunday School class is so popular that kids hate to miss it and parents rave about it. After hearing about her class and then visiting it several times, we begged Nancy to "write it down." Her methods and plans can be used and adapted by any teacher of 4th to 8th graders to keep them interested and growing spiritually. We wanted to make these wonderful lessons available to teachers everywhere. —The Publisher

Cover Design and Illustration by Beverly H. Hall

Item #308X— Paul's Journeys Lesson Guide
ISBN 1-890947-00-8
Copyright © 1997 Rose Publishing
4455 Torrance Blvd. Suite 259, Torrance, CA 90503
All rights reserved—Printed in the U.S.A.

05

Paul's Journeys: Then and Now

The 20"x26" Paul's Journeys: Then and Now (#304) map can be posted in your class. Reproduce individual copies from the masters on page 39-40. A giant wall map can be outlined on a bed sheet taped to the wall. Project the map with an overhead projector. You can make your own transparency or buy Rose Publishing's "Then and Now Bible Map Transparencies", (#307X) which have modern day overlays to use over the Bible map transparencies so students can see where the Bible locations are today. For every lesson, mark the day's Port of Call on the map with a red dot or move a toy boat to the next port.

Notes

Each lesson contains treats, souvenirs and crafts that Nancy has used in her classes. Choose which options you'd like to use for each lesson. Treats and crafts help students remember the lesson and make them look forward to the class. When students enjoy class, discipline is less of an issue. Nancy and her teaching staff are always looking for bargains on supplies for future lessons. They buy the items themselves, but you could ask parents for donations of treats or souvenirs that are meaningful to the lesson. A partial list is included in the cruise brochure. Send home your needs list before you start the unit. Some businesses will donate coupons or favors that can be used in the souvenir shop.

Mediterranean Cruise Adventure

Visit 12 Ports of Call with the Apostle Paul! Goal: To discover new life in Jesus Christ, to see Paul's changed life, and to realize the need to tell the world the Good News. Here are 12 detailed, step-by-step lesson plans for a "cruise" to the cities Paul visited on his journeys in Acts. The overview on pages 4-5 shows all twelve lessons, the city you will visit each week, the theme, Bible text, projects, and options. Decide which options to use with each lesson. You might call your unit "CLUB MED" or some other catchy title. Start planning your cruise today!

ROOM ENVIRONMENT

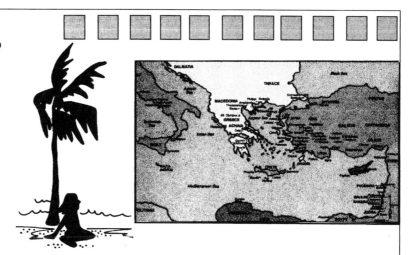

Wall Map: Enlarge the individual map of Paul's journeys on to a flat bed sheet using an overhead projector. Outline the shore line with paint and write place names with markers.

Palm Tree: For a quick, life-size palm tree, open brown paper bags, crumple and tape or staple to wall to form tree trunk. Cut branches from green construction paper.

Port Signs: Print city signs on bright paper and post on wall above map. (See page 37.)

Miscellaneous: Possible items to post include: the Bible passages; travel posters of the Mediterranean; photos or post cards (or color copies) of Israel, Greece, and Rome; and Hebrew and Greek alphabets.

ADVENTURE LAY-OUT

Pages 4 and 5 illustrate the lessons and extras

Weekly Lessons have a Port of Call number.
Weekly themes are based on the text.
Memory Scripture There are three Scripture passages. Each one is repeated four times.
Journeys Refer to four of Paul's journeys (listed on the back of *Paul's Journeys* wall chart.)
City refers to the weekly Port of Call.
Lifestyle/Attitude refers to the attitude of the general population in each Port of Call.
Passport Stamp There is a space for each Port of Call on students' passports. Rubber stamps can be used to mark attendance each week.
Weekly Craft or Project A suggestion is included for each lesson.
Weekly Souvenir A suggestion for each lesson.
Weekly Treat A suggestion for each lesson.
Special Ideas for occasional specials or guests are noted on the Port of Call pages and other places throughout the book.
Xtra Extra activities to make the cruise fun and exciting include learning a little Hebrew and Greek, pool parties, breakfast in class, and an evening buffet.
Meddie The mischievous Loch Med Monster and MC (monster catcher) are included to add some drama to the adventure. See pages 6 and 37.

A LESSON

Based on an average class of one hour, the following suggested sample lesson may be helpful. Adjust time for your class. Each lesson can be split into two 40 minute classes.

Pre-session 15 minutes
Students can learn and say the memory verse, work on the foreign language, stamp passports, and start the craft project.

Lesson and Application 30 minutes
Motivate students to take their seats for the lesson by offering Med Money. Present the lesson. Allow time at the end to discuss application for today.

Craft 15 minutes
It's best to do the craft at the end of the hour if possible. In classes where students do not all arrive on time it may be better to do the craft first. Unfinished crafts may be completed at home.

Before students leave, hand out treats and souvenirs with a reminder of the key point of the lesson.

IN EVERY LESSON be sure to include the message of salvation through the life, death, and resurrection of Jesus Christ as proclaimed in the Bible lessons. Offer students the opportunity to respond to the Gospel and accept Jesus as their Savior.

MEDITERRANEAN CRUISE

	PORT OF CALL	PORT CITY	THEME	TEXT	MEMORY SCRIPTURE	Attitude of City	Project Craft
Paul's First Journey	1	Antioch p.11-12	Respect	Acts 13	I Peter 3:15	Eager for God's Word	Passport — Map
	2	Galatia p.13-14	Fruit of the Spirit	Galatians 5	I Peter 3:15	Opposed/ Hostile to God's Word	Wallet
	3	Philippi p.15-17	Devotion	Acts 16:11-40	I Peter 3:15	Occult	Key Chain
Paul's Second Journey	4	Thessa-lonica p.19-20	Light	Acts 17	I Peter 3:15	Indifferent (mob rule)	Travel Bag
	5	Corinth p.21-22	Giving	II Corinthians 8,9	II Corinthians 9:6 Galatians 6:7,9	Immoral	Camera
	6	Athens p.23-24,18	Prepar-ation	Ephesians 6	II Corinthians 9:6 Galatians 6:7,9	Religious	Armor Picture — T-Shirt
	7	Ephesus p.25-27,18	Hope	Acts 19	II Corinthians 9:6 Galatians 6:7,9	Money Minded	Armor Picture
Paul's Third Journey	8	Macedonia p.28, 18	Love	Acts 20	II Corinthians 9:6 Galatians 6:7,9	Missionary Minded	Armor Picture — Mug
	9	Jerusalem p.29-30	Wisdom	Acts 21,22	Philippians 4:4-7, 13	Traditional Legalistic	Fish Magnet
	10	Caesarea p.31-32	Faith	Acts 22:30-Acts 26	Philippians 4:4-7, 13	Peaceful, Prosperous	Water Bottle Holder
Paul's Journey to Rome	11	Malta p.33-34	Courage	Acts 27-28:10	Philippians 4:4-7, 13	Generous, Kind	Hat/Visor
	12	Rome p.35-36	Truth	Acts 28	Philippians 4:4-7, 13	Pagan	

12-LESSON OVERVIEW

SOUVENIR	TREAT	SPECIAL ACTIVITY	XTRA	ADDITIONAL SUPPLIES
Cup, Ice Cream Dish	Coffee Can Ice Cream	Travel Brochure	Hebrew	*Camera, passport materials, passport stamps, (every week)* 3 lb. coffee can, ingredients
Fruit Magnet	Candy Fruit	Fruit Basket Game	Hebrew — Sun-Up Breakfast	Wallet materials, strip magnets, magazines, dice, fruit pictures, breakfast, invitations for pool party
Sun Glasses	Life Savers	Life Boat Drill	Hebrew — Pool Party	Key rings, beads, lacing, quiz sheets
Stone-Shaped Balls	"Stone" Jelly Beans	Shuffle Board	Hebrew	Shopping bags, markers, paper & glue, shuffleboard, invitation to Dessert Theatre
Pencil	Seeds	Missionary	Hebrew — Dessert Theatre	Pens or pencils, Missionary, film canisters, cereal boxes, paint, ears of corn
Shoe Laces	Watermelon	Seed Spitting	Greek	Armor prop, watermelon, shoe laces, t-shirts
Sand Dollar	Dollar Cookies Gold Coins	Bingo	Greek — Pool Party	Sand dollars, bingo game, copies of script, "microphones"
	Fish Cookies/ Crackers	Missionary	Greek — Sun-Up Breakfast	Breakfast, mugs, signs, props, missionary
	Fish (sticks)	Cook-out	Greek	B-B-Q, charcoal, fish sticks, fabric, magnets, fish crackers, suitcase, props
Water Bottle		Quoits	Greek	Bottles of water, cord, quoits, chalk, string
	Gummie Snakes	Storm	Greek	Props for the skit, blue blanket, boxes, sword rubber snake, invitation to buffet
Souvenir Shop	Party		Greek — Late Night Buffet	Objects for object lesson, souvenir shop items

Cruise Brochure

Design and photocopy a calendar and/or a cruise brochure for all class members. A brochure adds to the excitement and anticipation. Be sure to include all important information, such as,

shore excursions, Med money and extra activities. See pages 7-8.

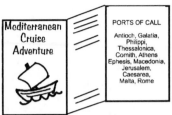

MED MONEY

Med Money is a great incentive for getting and keeping students excited about the activities and lessons on the cruise. Use play money or use page 10. Use it throughout the cruise as awards for: attendance, bringing a Bible, memorizing Scripture and other "good deeds" of your choosing. Med Money is the only legal tender at the Souvenir Shop you will set up at the end of the cruise. Students are responsible for keeping their own Med Money from class to class. It's as valuable as cash and students should be encouraged to take care of it. A good craft project for the beginning of the cruise is to make a wallet. Also students may want to write their name or initials on their Med Money for easy recognition.

PASSPORTS

Use passports to connect your lessons from port to port. Newcomers can make passports upon arrival. Passport photos can be taken using Polaroid or regular film. Try to get two individuals in each shot and cut the photo in two. Passports are stamped at the beginning of each session. Purchase stamps or cut your own from a potato in shapes such as a cross or a fish. On the back of the passport students can write their names in Hebrew and Greek which were the languages in use in Bible times. One challenge with these languages is that the English alphabet contains letters and sounds not included in either Hebrew or Greek and phonetic substitutions need to be used. Another challenge is that Hebrew is written from right to left and the alphabet contains only consonants. Rubber stamps are available for both alphabets, but attempting to form the characters free hand will give the students a feeling of accomplishment: see page 9.

MORE MAPS

Individual maps of Paul's journeys can be reproduced from the master on pages 39-40 to follow the progress of each journey. Water base markers may be used on colored laminated maps of Paul's journeys and then washed off. Students can create a relief map to illustrate hills, valleys, seashore, bodies of water and islands. A dough made from one part salt and four parts flour (with enough water to make a stiff dough). The dough works well on plywood. The dough will air dry in about a week depending on its thickness and can be painted with acrylic or poster paint.

Photos

Assign a helper or student to take pictures of activities in each port of call to be used for a slide show or scrap book at the end of the cruise. See page 28.

Meddie

Here is a special feature that you may choose to include in your cruise. The Loch Med Monster, also known as Meddie, is a fictional character designed after the Loch Ness Monster (Nessie) in Scotland. Meddie Catcher or MC is a real life character who is in hot pursuit of Meddie. MC can be a teen or adult who will play the part throughout your adventure. There is no script but the general idea is that MC is looking for Meddie because she has something or knows something that MC needs. MC drops in to class occasionally to request the students' support in finding Meddie. Sometimes MC just leaves notes for the class because he is off following up on a new lead about Meddie's whereabouts. He (or she) can dress as an adventurer type, sort of "Indiana Jones" with a khaki vest and shorts, binoculars, camera and walking stick, or as Carmen Santiago. See script ideas on page 37.

SHORE EXCURSIONS

Events held outside of class time.

Ideas for shore excursions include: Pool party (public or private pool) with snacks, park or beach adventure including hike, games and possibly a cook-out, local jail, boat trip, dramatic theater production and silversmith. Possibilities are limited only by your imagination and resources.

Use the ready-made shore excursion ticket on pages 7-8. Add date, time, destination, cost and any other necessary details. The reverse side is a permission-emergency form to be signed and returned by parents. Tickets should be distributed several weeks prior to the event. Publicity for events which will occur at the regular meeting place may also prove effective. Once the cruise has begun have students design flyers and posters for publicity.

Mediterranean Cruise Adventure

SOUVENIR SHOP

We need inexpensive gifts or souvenirs donated for our shop. Students will use the Med Money they earn on the cruise to purchase souvenirs at the end of the cruise.

The Souvenir Shop will be open on:

Students are responsible for bringing their Med Money on the above noted date. Med Money is the only legal tender in the Souvenir Shop.

Permission Slip / Emergency Form

_____ (name)
has my permission to attend the activity described on the reverse side. Emergency phone number:

_____
_____
Parent signature   date

Permission Slip / Emergency Form

_____ (name)
has my permission to attend the activity described on the reverse side. Emergency phone number::

_____
_____
Parent signature   date

Dear Parents,

Keep this cruise brochure to help you follow our class adventure for 12 weeks.

Your student will earn Med Money for: bringing his/her own Bible to class, memorizing Scripture, helping with a service or mission project, participating in class.

Sun-Up Breakfast: On _____

and _____ we will prepare and serve breakfast to all students who arrive one half hour early for class.

"Shore excursions" outside of class time: Our plans include a Pool Party on

(Be sure to sign the permission slip on the back of the ticket so your child can participate.)

And, an Evening Buffet on

Family and friends are invited to accompany students for a potluck buffet and special program about our cruise adventure.

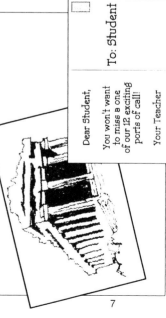

Dear Student,

You won't want to miss a one of our 12 exciting ports of call!

Your Teacher

To: Student

Needs List

Here's an opportunity for you to participate in the special activities of our class. We could use the following donations for projects, excursions and souvenir shop.

35mm slide film
empty coffee cans with lids
plastic cups
fruit magnets
hollow plastic or straw fruit
wallet kits
sun glasses
Life Saver candy
key rings
shuffleboard game
plain shopping bags
new pens or pencils
peanuts/snacks/treats
sunflower seeds
roasted pumpkin seeds
watermelon
gummy snacks
shoe laces
new t-shirts
fabric paint
markers
sand dollars
strip magnets

For our excursions and special events we could use:

a swimming pool
tickets to a play
BBQ area and grill

Please call to donate these or other items you may have.

Memory Verses

Weeks 1-4: I Peter 3:15

Weeks 5-8: II Corinthians 9:6
Galatians 6:7,9

Weeks 9-12: Philippians 4:4-7, 13

These verses support the theme of our cruise lessons and we will be encouraging the students to memorize them. As an incentive we will be awarding Med Money each week for every verse recited. Please join us in this effort and work on memorizing the verses at home.

ONE TICKET
EVENING BUFFET

_____ (date)

_____ (time)

Admit one student and student's family and friends.

SHORE EXCURSION TICKET

(event) _____

Date: _____

Time: _____

Good for: _____

PORTS OF CALL

DATE	PORT
_____	Antioch
_____	Galatia
_____	Philippi
_____	Thessalonica
_____	Corinth
_____	Athens
_____	Ephesus
_____	Macedonia
_____	Jerusalem
_____	Caesarea
_____	Malta
_____	Rome

Cut on dotted lines. Glue first panel on the outside of folded, blue construction paper (approx. 9"x9").
Cut out and glue the other two panels on the inside to form a passport.

Antioch	Galatia	Philippi
Thessa-lonica	Corinth	Athens
Ephesus	Macedonia	Jerusalem
Caesarea	Malta	Rome

Paste photo here

Name: _____

Address: _____

_____

Phone: _____

Birthdate: _____

Teacher: See directions on Page 6.

PASSPORT

Date: _____

MED MONEY Photocopy this page of Med Money (Med stands for Mediterranean) on green paper and use as incentives for attendance, bringing a Bible, memorizing Scripture, and other "good deeds" of your choosing.

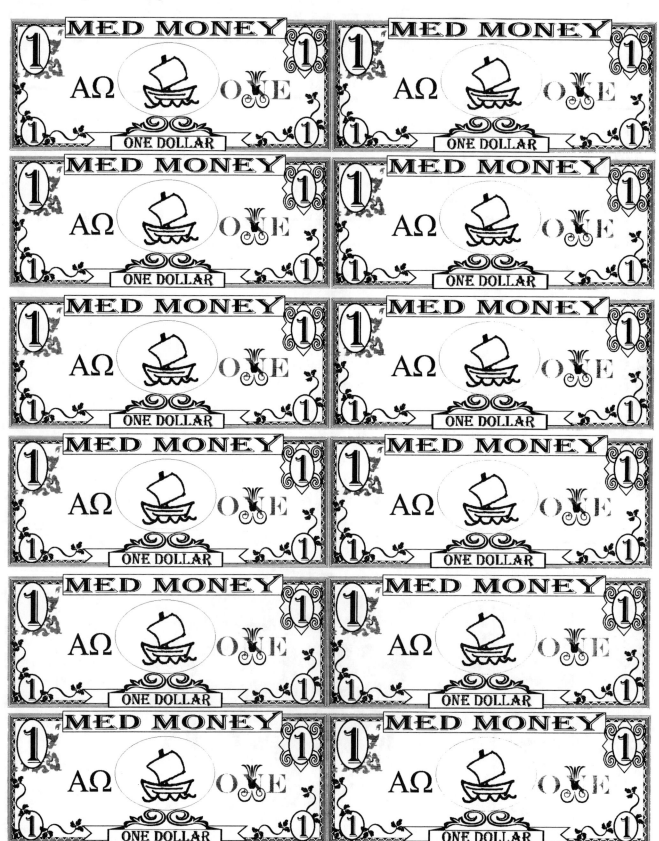

Port of Call #1

ANTIOCH

JOURNEY I

MEMORY VERSE

But in your hearts set apart Christ as Lord. Always be prepared to give an answer to everyone who asks you to give the reason for the hope that you have. But do this with gentleness and respect.

I Peter 3:15
(NIV)

TREAT: COFFEE CAN ICE CREAM

Historically the invention of ice cream is attributed to the Romans. Here's a fun way to make and share this special treat.

The class works together to make the ice cream by rolling the coffee can(s) across the floor to each other for about 10 minutes. Mix together in a bowl: ½ cup whipping cream, 1 cup milk; ¼ cup sugar; 1 teaspoon vanilla. Carefully pour into a zip lock bag and seal bag. Place chipped ice and about ½ cup salt in a 3 pound coffee can. Insert baggie into coffee can and add more ice and salt. Tape lid securely. Roll can on floor until ice cream is firm. One can feeds about six.

LOCH MED MONSTER

First skit to introduce Meddie and M.C. (see pages 6 and 37.)

CITY INFORMATION:

This city is sometimes called Antioch of Syria in order to distinguish it from the other 15 cities named Antioch. It was the third largest city in the Roman Empire with 500,000-800,000 residents. Walls divided it into four sections: Greek, Syrian, African and Jewish. Antioch was noted for its political power, trade and commerce, intellectual life and religious tolerance. Antioch is the city where followers of the Way were first called Christians (Acts 11:26) and it served as the headquarters for the early church. Today it is called Antakya in the country of Turkey. It is a town with a population of about 35,000.

LANGUAGE: HEBREW

Students are challenged to write their own name on the back of their passport in Hebrew (see Hebrew alphabet page 38.) They may also enjoy trying to translate the weekly word:

SHALOM

Pronounced *"sha-lowm"*, it literally means "peace." Shalom is commonly used as a greeting such as hello and good-bye.

SOUVENIR:

Plastic cup or ice cream dish with Club Med lettered on the side with permanent marker.

PROJECT: MAKE PASSPORTS

See page 9. Stamp Antioch today.

(outside)   (inside)

PASSPORT

cover

Name
_____

Antioch	Galatia	Philippi
Thess-alonica	Corinth	Athens
Ephesus	Mace-donia	Jeru-salem
Caesar-ea	Malta	Rome

Map labels: Iconium, CILICIA, Derbe, Tarsus, PAMPHYLIA, Antioch, Seleucia, SYRIA, CYPRUS, Salamis, Damascus, Sidon

LESSON 1 — ANTIOCH

THEME: Respect

GOAL: Discuss how respect was important in Paul's ministry. How is it important to the cause of Christ? How can we include respect in our lives? We treat others with respect even if we don't agree with them.

BIBLE: Acts 13

A brief summary about the Apostle Paul, his early life and his conversion is important for this series of lessons on his journeys.

Saul of Tarsus was a Pharisee (Philippians 3:4-6). He did not believe that Jesus was God and he hated Christians. He was present at the stoning of Stephen. He headed for Damascus to arrest Christians, but Jesus met him on the road and Saul became a believer (Acts 7-9). On Cyprus, Saul began using the Greek form of his name, Paul.

A chronological account of Paul's missionary journeys begins in the book of Acts, chapter 13. Have a brief class discussion before opening the text to help establish a foundation for the unit.

Choose to discuss some or all of the following questions. These questions can be reviewed and discussed several times during the cruise.

Who wrote the Book of Acts and why?
Luke recorded the spread of the Gospel throughout Asia and into Europe by the Apostles, so that everyone could see how God was establishing His Church.
What is a missionary? *Someone who tells others about salvation through Jesus Christ.*
Why tell others about Jesus? *Because Jesus told us to, Matthew 28:18.*
What is a Christian? *Someone who puts their faith in Jesus as Lord and Savior, and imitates Jesus in their words and actions.*
What do missionaries do today? *They tell others about salvation in Jesus Christ. They often do this by establishing food banks, schools, and health programs.*

Can you remember telling someone about Jesus? What happened?

It is very important that the teacher read through the Bible passage several times for personal familiarity and understanding.

Tell the students that Antioch was a beautiful city in the mountains near the Syrian border in what is today Southern Turkey. The new church in Antioch was spreading the message of salvation to both Jew and Gentile. The leaders were told by the Holy Spirit that God had chosen Barnabas and Saul to carry the Good News of Jesus abroad. Upon arrival in a new city they visited the local synagogue first. The Jews already knew about God; they needed to know about Jesus, the Messiah.

ACTS 13: Have the students read the story and prepare to re-tell it in a fun way by drawing pictures. Divide the class into pairs or groups and pass out slips of paper with verses from Acts 13: 1-5, 6-8, 9-12, 13-19, 20-25, 26-29, 30-37, 38-41, and 48-52. Depending on the size of your class, groups may have more than one Scripture assignment. Teachers may also choose to participate.

Instructions to small groups: Read the passage in the Bible and draw a picture (create a line drawing) of the action. Each group will have one minute to explain their passage and drawing to the total class.

Allow groups about 10 minutes to prepare and then share the drawings in verse order. Add any necessary comments and summarize the events of Chapter 13. Be sure to point out place locations on the wall map.

1-5 Barnabas and Saul arrive in Cyprus.
6-8 They travel the island and meet Elymas, a sorcerer and attendant to the proconsul, Sergius Paulus.
9-12 Saul is now Paul: he confronts Elymas.
13-19 They travel to Pisidian Antioch.
20-25 Paul retells God's message.
26-29 Paul tells about Jesus.
30-37 God raised Jesus from the dead!
38-41 Forgiveness of sin.
42-47 The whole city cames to hear Paul, but some Jews become abusive. Paul and Barnabas remain calm and respectful.
48-52 Jews stir up persecution and have Paul and Barnabas expelled.

✱ Sun-Up Breakfast next week! ✱

MEMORY VERSE

But in your hearts set apart Christ as Lord. Always be prepared to give an answer to everyone who asks you to give the reason for the hope that you have. But do this with gentleness and respect.

I Peter 3:15 (NIV)

ACTIVITY: FRUIT BASKET GAME

Purchase 4-6 hollow plastic or straw fruits that can be opened and closed. (Or allow time to make some out of small boxes covered in colored paper.) Put small surprises in each fruit. Make 1 or 2 dice with a different color on each side, corresponding to the fruit "boxes", usually red, orange, yellow, green, purple and/or brown. Divide class into teams, or play as individuals. Make up review questions for last week's lesson. A right answer earns the opportunity to roll the dice. Winners get to choose a small surprise from the fruit corresponding to the color showing on the dice.

TREAT:

Fruit candy such as Runts® or fruit snack.

SOUVENIR:

Fruit magnet to remind students of the Fruit of the Spirit. Fruit magnets may be purchased at a craft store or made by gluing pictures of fruit to magnets.

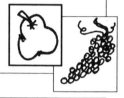

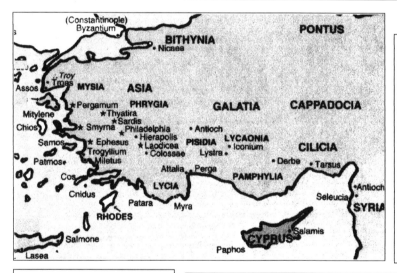

AREA INFORMATION:

Galatia is a plateau region in central Asia Minor. The name is from the Celtic tribes from Gaul (France) who were driven east and settled in the area in the Third Century BC. The cities of Galatia had no walls so citizens could easily escape to the nearby mountains for safety. Galatia was conquered by Rome in 166 BC. North Galatia kept its own Celtic language and gods, but South Galatia adopted the cult of emperor worship. Judaism existed in Galatia for centuries after Christ.

LANGUAGE: HEBREW

This weeks words to translate are:

TORAH

Pronounced *"Toe-rah"*, it means the "Law".

JERUSALEM

Pronounced *"Yaru-salem"*, loosely translated it means "city of peace."

CRAFT: Wallet

Class members will be earning lots of Med Money and a wallet will help them keep it in one place until they get a chance to spend it at the Souvenir Shop. Purchased wallet kits are available from craft supply stores. A simple wallet can be made from legal size envelopes. Just fold in the flap and glue it down, then fold it in half to look like a wallet. Wallets could also be made from felt and decorated with puffy paint.

SPECIAL: *Sun-Up* Breakfast on Deck

A popular, early morning activity on cruise ships is breakfast on deck. A simple breakfast before class can be a special treat.
MENU: WAFFLES, use the frozen kind and heat up in a toaster. WHIPPED TOPPING, use frozen or spray can. STRAWBERRIES, thaw out frozen berries. JUICE, add water to frozen concentrate.

LESSON 2 GALATIA

THEME: The Fruit of the Spirit

GOAL: Discuss the difference between human emotions and the attributes of God. The presence of God's Spirit in our lives should make a noticeable difference to our friends and families.

BIBLE: Acts 14

Tell the students: Galatia was an area of Asia Minor in what is now part of the country of Turkey. Find it on the map. Stamp your passport for Galatia.

Acts 14 details the experiences of Paul and Barnabas on the last half of their first missionary journey.

In Iconium, many Jews and Gentiles listened to Paul preach and believed in Jesus. The Jews who refused to believe stirred up the city against them. Paul and Barnabas explained the Gospel clearly and God confirmed their teaching with miracles.

When Paul and Barnabas found out about a plot to stone them, they left town and headed for Lystra.

After Paul and Barnabas healed a lame man in Lystra, the people called them gods. Paul protested strongly and tried to explain God's plan to the people. Some Jews from Antioch and Iconium turned the people against Paul. The crowd stoned him and dragged him outside of the city, thinking he was dead.

Paul survived his injuries. He and Barnabas headed for the city of Derbe. He preached in Derbe and a lot of people believed in Christ.

Paul and Barnabas revisited the Galatian cities where they found small groups of believers in each city. They appointed elders for the new churches and encouraged them. After traveling to Attalia they sailed back to Antioch.

Later in Paul's travels he wrote a letter to the churches in Galatia challenging them to remain faithful to the Gospel of Christ and to live a life honoring to God.

After warning them about acting out their sin nature, Paul described the result of a life controlled by the Spirit of God. The fruit of the Spirit is produced in the lives of believers (Galatians 5:22-23).

Paul uses an effective word picture when he tells the Galatians about the fruit of the Spirit. The good fruit produced in a person's life is the evidence of the presence of God's Spirit. Equally apparent is the bad fruit produced by a person being controlled by fallen human nature.

Paul lists LOVE first. After evaluating the entire passage, it can be said that love is the fruit of the Spirit and the other attributes are a result of God's love. Of course it can also be said that love is just the first of nine attributes of God. Whichever approach you take, these are supernatural attitudes in a believer's life. They are not produced or controlled by human means.

LOVE - αγαπε (agapé) is unselfish, always doing what is best for another person.

JOY is not an emotion. We may be happy or sad, but joy is the confidence that God cares about us — no matter what.

PEACE is not the absence of conflict. Peace is knowing that God is in control.

PATIENCE is the ability to put up with any situation.

KINDNESS is demonstrating our concern for others.

GOODNESS is doing the right thing no matter what consequences occur.

FAITHFULNESS is being trustworthy and dependable, true to your word.

GENTLENESS is being fair and caring for the feelings of others.

SELF-CONTROL is being in control of your thoughts as well as your actions.

DISCUSSION QUESTIONS OR QUICK-WRITE: (5 minutes)

How would the world be different without the fruit of the Spirit?

How would your life be different if you were really producing the fruit of the Spirit?

Send home Pool Party information for next week.

14

MEMORY VERSE

But in your hearts set apart Christ as Lord. Always be prepared to give an answer to everyone who asks you to give the reason for the hope that you have. But do this with gentleness and respect.

I Peter 3:15 (NIV)

ACTIVITY: LIFE BOAT DRILL

A very important activity on a cruise ship is the life boat drill when everyone puts on their life vest and finds the life boat they are assigned to. Teach your class the procedure to follow to exit the building in case of emergency, fire, earthquake, etc. Have someone ring a bell and announce the drill.

TREAT
Life Savers® candy

SOUVENIR
Sunglasses. Often children's sunglasses are inexpensive at discount stores or through mail order. Or make your own from cardboard and cellophane. They remind us of the Mediterranean sunshine and our cruise adventure.

Reference Scripture verses for key chain.

GOLD: Philippians 3:20

BLUE: Psalm 90:2

BLACK: Romans 3:23

RED: John 3:16

WHITE: Isaiah 1:18

GREEN: II Peter 3:18

AREA INFORMATION:

Philippi was a Roman colony in Eastern Macedonia, about 10 miles inland. It was founded in 356 BC by the Macedonian King Philip, father of Alexander the Great. The name means "city of Philip." At the time it had vast gold and silver mines. It served as the gateway to Greece and Italy as much of the traffic to Rome from the east traveled through Philippi. There may have been no synagogue in the city, since only a small group of believers, mostly women, met by the river for worship.

LANGUAGE: HEBREW
This week's words to translate are:

HALLELUJAH
Pronounced *"ha-lay-lu-yah"*, it literally means "praise the Lord!"

ISRAEL
Pronounced *"ees-ra-el"*, it means "contended with God"

CRAFT: SALVATION KEY CHAIN
Make a key ring to tell the plan of salvation.
Supplies needed: Purchased key rings, colored plastic or wooden beads (gold, blue, black, red, white, green), leather or plastic lacing. Each student should attach the beads in order to the lacing and then attach the lacing to the key ring. When someone asks about the beads, it is an opportunity to tell that the **gold** bead stands for heaven which is our real home; **blue** is for God's holiness; **black** reminds us that we are separated from God by sin; **red** represents Jesus' sacrifice on the cross to pay for our sin; **white** shows that our sins are washed whiter than snow, and **green** encourages us to grow in our faith.

SPECIAL: POOL PARTY
Even if you use a wading pool, your class will enjoy an afternoon splashing around the pool together. If you don't have a pool yourself, one of your students probably knows someone who will let you enjoy a dip. Remember to have several adult swimmers in attendance for safety. Send instructions and information home the week before the party. Remind students to bring permission slips. (p 7-8)

LESSON 3 PHILIPPI

THEME: Devotion

GOAL: Consider what it means to be devoted to God or devoted to evil. Discuss God's faithfulness and godly submission to authority.

BIBLE: Acts 16:11-40

Read Acts 16:11-40 to the class.
Trace Paul's journey in verses 11-12 on a map.
Stamp passports for Philippi.

Pass out quiz sheets to be worked on by students in pairs using their Bibles. This will get the students involved in the action and ready for a class discussion.

QUIZ ANSWERS

1. Tell two things about Philippi.
(It was a Roman colony. It was a leading city in Macedonia.)
2. What did Paul do on the Sabbath?
(Went outside the city gate to the river to find a place of prayer.)
3. Who did he find at the river? *(Women)*
4. Tell four things about Lydia.
(A dealer in purple cloth. From Thyatira. She worshipped God. She responded to Paul's message.) (Teachers note: You may want to look up the significance of purple cloth in a Bible dictionary.)
5. What was significant about the slave girl?
(She had a spirit that predicted the future. She earned money for her owners.)
6. Why did the slave girl follow Paul?
(To testify to the Spirit of God. She had a demon who spoke enough truth (v.17) to get people to believe lies. Satan has a lot of truth mixed with a great deal of lies.)
7. How did Paul respond to the slave girl?
(He cast out the evil spirit.)
8. What did the slave owners do?
(Seized Paul and Silas and took them to the authorities. They lied about what Paul did.)
9. What did the authorities do? *(They had Paul and Silas beaten and thrown into prison.)*
10. Describe the prison.
(Inner cell with stocks for prisoner's feet.)
11. How did Paul and Silas react?
(They prayed and sang hymns to God.)
12. What happened at midnight?
(A violent earthquake.)
13. What happened to the prison doors?
(They flew open.)

14. Why was the jailer going to kill himself?
(He thought the prisoners had escaped.)
15. What did the jailer ask Paul?
(What must I do to be saved?)
16. How did the jailer respond?
(He believed and was baptized with his family, he washed Paul and Silas's wounds and took them to his home and fed them. He was filled with joy.)
17. Why wouldn't Paul and Silas leave jail?
(They wanted the authorities to escort them. They wanted to submit to prison authorities so there would be no doubt of how they got out.)
18. How did the authorities react to the news that Paul was a Roman citizen? *(With alarm!)*
19. Where did Paul and Silas go after they left prison? *(To Lydia's house.)*

After the class has finished the quiz, gather in one group. Have 2 or 3 good readers read the passage aloud. Share some individual student's answers and then encourage the students to discuss some of these issues.

● Paul's travels in vs 11-12 take him from Asia Minor to Europe for the first time. Why is this important? *God's Truth was spreading from East and penetrating Greek and Roman cultures.*

● Worshippers of God met outside the city near the river indicating that there probably wasn't a synagogue in Philippi. As a dealer in purple cloth, Lydia was probably very wealthy. Purple dye was very expensive; therefore purple cloth could only be afforded by the rich.

● The slave girl had an evil spirit which allowed her to predict the future and earn a lot of money for her owners. Having an evil spirit is not good; earning a lot of money might be good. Paul got rid of the evil spirit and the owner's response landed Paul and Silas in prison. Why would the crowd join in against Paul? *They probably didn't care about the girl, but they selfishly cared a lot about her ability to predict the future.*

● Stripped, beaten, flogged and put in stocks are serious consequences for doing a good thing! Have you ever heard about someone getting in trouble for doing something good? How would the average person react to a beating, prison and stocks? How could Paul and Silas sing and pray? How do you think that affected the other prisoners?

● What would the average person do if the prison doors flew open? Paul's unusual response deeply affected the jailer.

Have you ever heard about something good coming out of something bad?
What does this tell us about God? *(He is faithful.)*
How can Paul's example help us when we face difficult situations? *(We can trust God to work it out.)*

? Why do you think we are having Lifesaver treats today? *To remind us that Jesus is our lifesaver. He saved us!*

PAUL'S ADVENTURE IN PHILIPPI

Two people work together.
Find a partner and read: Acts 16:11-40.
Fill in the answers to the following questions.
Some teams will be able to share their answers with the class.

1. Tell two things about Philippi.

2. What did Paul do on the Sabbath?

3. Who did he find at the river?

4. Tell four things about Lydia.

5. What was significant about the slave girl?

6. Why did the slave girl follow Paul?

7. How did Paul respond to the slave girl?

8. What did the slave owners do?

9. What did the authorities do?

10. Describe the prison.

11. How did Paul and Silas react?

12. What happened at midnight?

13. What happened to the prison doors?

14. Why was the jailer going to kill himself?

15. What did the jailer ask Paul?

16. How did the jailer respond?

17. Why wouldn't Paul and Silas leave jail?

18. How did the authorities react to the news that Paul was a Roman citizen?

19. Where did Paul and Silas go after they left prison?

THE ARMOR OF GOD   EPHESIANS 6:10-16

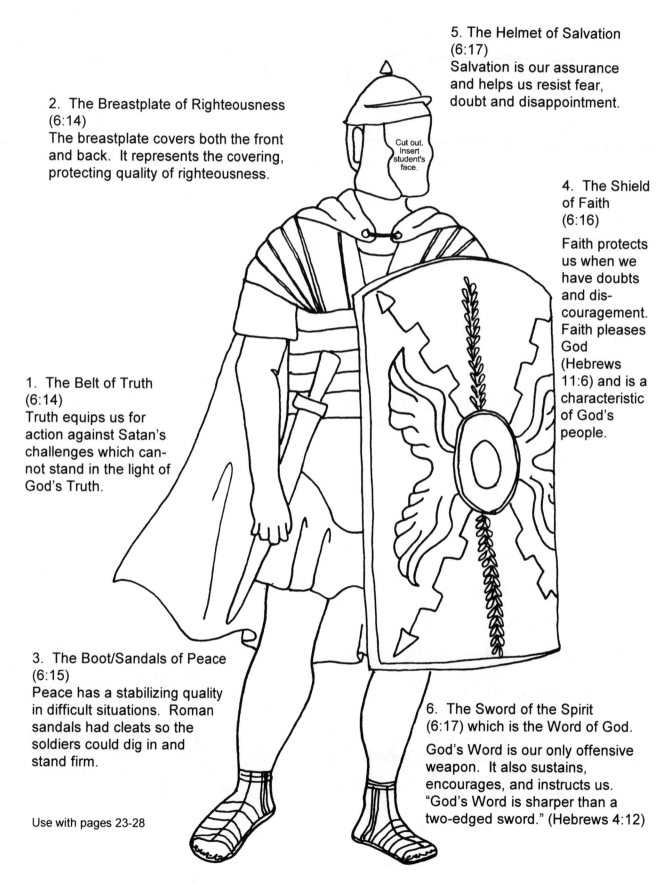

5. The Helmet of Salvation (6:17)
Salvation is our assurance and helps us resist fear, doubt and disappointment.

2. The Breastplate of Righteousness (6:14)
The breastplate covers both the front and back. It represents the covering, protecting quality of righteousness.

Cut out. Insert student's face.

4. The Shield of Faith (6:16)
Faith protects us when we have doubts and dis-couragement. Faith pleases God (Hebrews 11:6) and is a characteristic of God's people.

1. The Belt of Truth (6:14)
Truth equips us for action against Satan's challenges which can-not stand in the light of God's Truth.

3. The Boot/Sandals of Peace (6:15)
Peace has a stabilizing quality in difficult situations. Roman sandals had cleats so the soldiers could dig in and stand firm.

6. The Sword of the Spirit (6:17) which is the Word of God.
God's Word is our only offensive weapon. It also sustains, encourages, and instructs us. "God's Word is sharper than a two-edged sword." (Hebrews 4:12)

Use with pages 23-28

MEMORY VERSE

But in your hearts set apart Christ as Lord. Always be prepared to give an answer to everyone who asks you to give the reason for the hope that you have. But do this with gentleness and respect.

I Peter 3:15
(NIV)

ACTIVITY/CRAFT: Travel Bag

Travel bags are a useful item to have on any trip, including cruises, to hold personal items. Bags may be made of fabric, plastic or paper and they may be purchased ready made or constructed by you and your staff. Students need to begin with a finished bag so they can spend their time decorating it.

Depending on the basic material, decorations may be added with craft paint, markers, iron on fabric designs, paper and glue.

TREAT

Stone jelly beans.

(Brach's® Candy Co. makes jelly beans that look like rocks.)

SOUVENIR

Balls that look like rocks.
(See page 38 for Oriental Trading Co. catalog.)
The treat and souvenir remind us of Paul's stoning.

MEDDIE:

It's time for another visit from MC.
If class time is short MC could arrive during the craft time and explain his latest adventure and discoveries concerning Meddie.
(see ideas on page 37)

LANGUAGE: HEBREW

This week's words to translate are:

MESSIAH
Pronounced *"ma-she-ah"*. In English it means "anointed one."

AMEN
Pronounced *"a-main'*. In English it means "so be it."

SPECIAL: SHUFFLEBOARD

A very popular activity on board cruise ships is a game of shuffleboard. Draw the target area on floor (or sidewalk or asphalt) with chalk or mark it with masking tape. Detailed information on the game is available in books on games or you can make up your own rules to fit your class and particular situation. If you have access to actual shuffleboard equipment, use it. If not, create your own. Hockey sticks and pucks can be substituted. You'll need one or two old broom (or mop) handles and several "pucks" (pebbles, jar lids, or checkers). Divide the class into teams and play several rounds. You may give small prizes for the winners or Med Money.

LESSON 4 THESSALONICA

THEME: Light

GOAL: Discuss how we can share our faith in the Light of the World, Jesus, in spite of opposition.

BIBLE: Acts 17

AREA INFORMATION:

Thessalonica was founded by King Cassander of Macedonia in 316 BC. It was granted free-city status by Rome. Thessalonica was located on a Roman road that ran across Macedonia from the Adriatic Sea to the Aegean Sea. It was a coastal, commercial city and an international port. Merchants and other travelers heading to Europe or Asia passed through Thessalonica. The highway and harbor brought commercial and military traffic through the city.

Briefly review Paul's experience in Philippi: He was beaten, thrown into prison, and survived an earthquake. Now in Acts 17 he heads south. Point to location on the map. This Port of Call is Thessalonica; however the lesson will also take us to Berea and Athens. Stamp your passport for Thessalonica.

Begin by dividing the class into four groups and assign a passage from Acts 17 to each group; verses 1-9 (Thessalonica), 10-15 (Berea), 16-23 and 32-34 (Athens), and 24-31 (Paul's speech). Each group is to read their passage and discuss these questions: What are the people in that city like? How did they treat Paul? What did they do with the Gospel?

After each group has reported on their city, discuss these questions: What's worse, being laughed at and not taken seriously or being stoned? How did Paul choose his tactics to suit the personality of each city? Why would someone walk 60 miles just to make trouble for Paul?

Other questions to consider. What are people like in your city? How do they treat Paul? What do they do with the Gospel?

Thessalonica: As an international sea port, Thessalonica was home to a varied population. Without even listening to Paul's words or evaluating their content, many decide he is a threat to their way of life and they determine to stop him. He manages to get out of town alive, but some Thessalonicans follow him all the way to Berea and make trouble for him there.

Berea: Sixty miles from Thessalonica, Berea was a small town with a much more homogeneous population. People listen to Paul with an open mind and then check out what he said. Many people place their faith in Christ because of Paul's preaching.

Athens: Athens was home to artisans, philosophers and thinkers. In general the

Atheneans celebrated the human mind. Greeks thought of the atom and the size and shape of the earth. They also discovered mathematical and geometric principles. Other accomplishments included music, theater, medicine, ethics, grammar and more.

Paul's presence is accepted in Athens. He is allowed to speak openly, but the Gospel he preaches is not taken seriously by most who hear him.

Paul's Speech: The Areopagus, also known as Mars Hill, at the base of the Acropolis, was a popular spot for public speakers. Paul begins his message by pointing out that he has observed how religious they were. He tells them they did not have to wonder about the "unknown god" any longer. He tells them about the God of the Bible and the hope of salvation through Jesus Christ, but most of the listeners just consider him one more philosopher in a city of philosophers. They don't beat him up or run him out of town, but very few take him very seriously either.

THINK ABOUT IT - TALK ABOUT IT

 You will find this bell symbol in two different places in this book. It will be attached to a box with some thought provoking questions. The questions have application with several of the different lessons. Use them as your time and interest permit when you plan your lesson, incorporate them in your application discussion, or even use them as take-home assignments.

—What distresses you spiritually about your city?
—Have you experienced an incorrect story told about you? What happened?
—What spiritual counterfeits have you noticed in modern culture?
—What do you appreciate most about being a citizen of your country? About being a citizen of God's kingdom?

MEMORY VERSE

Remember this: Whoever sows sparingly will also reap sparingly, and whoever sows generously will also reap generously.

Do not be deceived: God cannot be mocked. A man reaps what he sows. Let us not become weary in doing good, for at the proper time we will reap a harvest if we do not give up.

*II Corinthians 9:6
and Galatians 6: 7,9
(NIV)*

ACTIVITY: MISSIONS

After four weeks of learning about first century missionaries, it's time to discuss what's going on in the world today. There are an abundance of mission agencies worldwide, each with its own particular strategy on sharing the Gospel. Many provide schools, hospitals, food, clothing, and occupational training in remote and undeveloped areas of the world. Several continue to work on Bible translations. There are probably missionaries associated with your church who would be happy to visit your class and talk about their work. An alternative would be to show a short video in class about a current mission effort.

SOUVENIR

Pencils or pens are popular souvenirs, especially if you are able to have them imprinted or tape on a printed label. Remind students that the Apostle Paul wrote many letters of encouragement and instruction

LANGUAGE:
HEBREW

IMMANUEL
Pronounced *"em-man-u-el"*, it literally means "God with us."

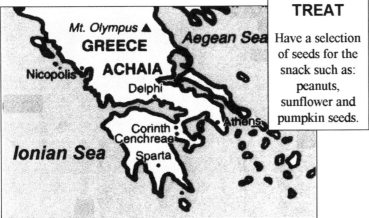

TREAT

Have a selection of seeds for the snack such as: peanuts, sunflower and pumpkin seeds.

AREA INFORMATION:

Corinth is located 2 miles inland from the Gulf of Corinth at the foot of Acrocorinth, a 1,886 foot hill which dominates the city. A temple of Aphrodite, the goddess of love, was situated on top. Corinth was known as the "city of shopkeepers." The main road leading to the agora (market) was 25 feet wide and made of limestone. The entrance was a broad staircase and gateway. A synagogue was nearby.

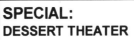

CRAFT:

One item you don't want to forget on any trip is your camera. A simple replica can be made using an individual-serving size cereal box and a 35mm film canister. Cut a hole in the front of the cereal box, then cover the box with black construction paper. Use chalk or paint to add details. Insert canister for the lens. Since the theme is giving and the camera isn't real it could be used as a bank to save money for missionaries. Or, cut a slit in the back and use it to store photos. It could also be weighted and used as a paper weight. Be sure to take real photos of the students and send them along with short messages of love and encouragement to missionaries supported by your church.

SPECIAL:
DESSERT THEATER

An exciting feature on cruise ships is the entertainment. Grand musical and theatrical productions are usually presented each evening. With a little planning, it is possible to find a production at a local school, community theatre or another church which would be appropriate for your class. Plan to take them out for dessert either before or after the "theater." Encourage students and volunteers to dress up for an evening out. Alternatives: A variety show with class members or show a good video.

LESSON 5 · CORINTH

<table>
<tr><td>

THEME: Giving

GOAL: Discuss how we can pursue the desire to be generous givers so that God can work through us in helping others.

BIBLE: II Corinthians 8,9

</td></tr>
</table>

Begin by reviewing the memory passage. Show the class a single kernel of corn and ask, "What kind of crop would you expect to result from that seed?" *(Possibly 5 or 6 ears of corn.)* Now show them several ears of corn or a large bag of seeds and ask the same question. *(Bushels and bushels, maybe a truckload, maybe more.)* Of course, the more seeds planted, the larger the harvest.

It's pretty easy to understand this principle when we're talking about seeds, so Paul used this illustration when he wrote to the Corinthians about financial matters.

Corinth was a wealthy city with a busy seaport and many shops. Most Corinthians were merchants or businessmen and financially secure.

The church in Jerusalem, on the other hand, was persecuted and desperately poor. The church in Macedonia was not much better off than Jerusalem, and yet the Macedonians begged Paul for the opportunity to give an offering for the Christians in Jerusalem.

In his second letter to the Corinthians, Paul used the Macedonian church as an example of the attitude of giving. Paul wanted to encourage the Corinthian believers to help other Christians. He also reminded them that Jesus had given everything to be born as a human and then to die for our sins.

Paul was very concerned about the attitude of giving. He wrote that God wants us to give freely of our time, our abilities and our money. He doesn't want us to have a grumbling or resentful attitude when we give. He wants us to be joyful. Paul assured the Corinthians that God provides for the needs of all who give generously.

Ask your guest missionary to share how important money and letters of support are to missionaries.

Discussion Questions:

Who is too poor to give? *No one.*

Name the two kinds of givers in II Corinthians 9:6 and the results of each attitude. *Sparing (not generous) givers with sparing returns and generous givers with generous returns.*

Ask students to tell about a time when they received or gave a generous gift. How did they feel? How did the other person feel?

What is the most generous gift God has given to us? *Jesus Christ.*

Why should we give? *God wants to bless others and he wants to use us to do it.*

Have each student think about people they could help by giving. Then have them decide on one and write down their plan for giving. (Be sure you know about projects sponsored by your church and suggest one to students having trouble thinking of one.)

Next, as a class, discuss a project you could give to. Be sure to invite your guest missionary to make some suggestions. Write up a class plan; assign specific responsibilities to students and set a deadline. For instance, one class in a beach city filled a beach bag for a South American orphanage to be delivered by a missionary. They included photos of the class and a single use camera so the recipients could take photos of themselves to send back to the class.

IMPORTANT INFORMATION

It is important to point out that Paul, Jesus' disciples and the majority of the early church were all faithful Jews. They recognized and accepted Jesus as the long awaited Messiah promised by God. As you read about Paul's journeys, you will note that he always went to the synagogue when he arrived in a new town. He preached the Gospel to the Jews first and many responded and accepted Jesus as Messiah and Savior.

The Jews who refused to believe Paul's message became a powerful opposition force. It is critical that these two groups are kept separate in discussing Paul's persecution.

First century Jewish believers did not become Gentiles. Today, as then, many Jews remain faithful to their tradition while accepting Jesus as their Messiah and completion of their faith.

MEMORY VERSE

Remember this: Whoever sows sparingly will also reap sparingly, and whoever sows generously will also reap generously.

Do not be deceived: God cannot be mocked. A man reaps what he sows. Let us not become weary in doing good, for at the proper time we will reap a harvest if we do not give up.

II Corinthians 9:6 and Galatians 6: 7,9 (NIV)

ACTIVITY:
ARMOR PICTURE

A visual way to remember the Armor of God is to "put" your students in the armor. Allow time for advance preparation. Project the picture of the Roman centurion (page 18) onto a large piece of butcher paper* (about 3'x6'). Copy and paint the centurion, cutting out a head-size hole where the face is. Secure the paper to a wood frame or large piece of cardboard (maybe a refrigerator carton). Take each student's picture with his/her face in the hole so they appear to be wearing the armor. When the photos are ready, have students glue them to heavy paper and write out Ephesians 6:10-17. *If you have the resources, you may choose to use stretched canvas instead of paper.

TREAT:
Watermelon, fresh or frozen.
Remember, you need the seeds for your "special."

SOUVENIR:
Today's souvenir is shoe laces to remind the students to lace up their shoes and get ready to share the Gospel of Peace. You may choose plain or colorful laces or even ones that say *"Jesus Loves You!"*

AREA INFORMATION:

Athens was the principal city of ancient Greece located 5 miles inland from the port of Piraeus. Athens was known as the city of learning. Philosophers spent time discussing the latest ideas. The agora (market), surrounded by public buildings, near the rocky hill called the Acropolis was a place for politics, commerce and social gatherings. The Parthenon, built on top of the Acropolis by Pericles in the fifth century BC honored Athena, the city's goddess whose magnificent statue faced the harbor. The Areopagus was a smaller hill named after the god of war, Ares, and was originally a meeting place for the city council and court. It is also known as Mars Hill. There was a synagogue near the agora.

LANGUAGE
GREEK

Now challenge students to write their name using Greek characters. (See alphabet on page 38)

This week's word to translate:

Aθενς

Athens

CRAFT: T-Shirts

A favorite keepsake from any trip is a t-shirt. There are several ways to create your own class t-shirts. (Begin by locating a supplier who will sell you seconds at a very low price.) Options:

- Allow students to design their own with fabric paint and permanent markers, or
- Have someone do a class design and trace it on each shirt, or
- Use a computer design printed on transfer paper and iron design onto t-shirts.
- Or, choose to do the t-shirts next week.

Design ideas: Tropical; List ports of call.

SPECIAL:
WATERMELON SEED SPITTING

This activity is just for fun. Save the seeds from the watermelon treat, 4 or 5 for each student. Draw large circle targets or use large hoops (indoors or outdoors). It works best if students can stand elevated above the target area, maybe even from the second floor. Students take turns spitting their seeds, aiming at the targets. Award ribbons, prizes, or Med Money to those who get the most seeds in the hoops.

LESSON 6

ATHENS

THEME: Preparation

GOAL: Prepare students to share the Gospel and to face spiritual warfare with God's protective armor.

BIBLE: Ephesians 6

Today our Port of Call is Athens and our Scripture is Ephesians 6. We visited Athens two lessons ago and we'll visit Ephesus next time, but Athens is too important to be left off of our passport. Be sure to stamp your passport!

Athens, along with the rest of the known world had been conquered by Rome. A lot of the credit for Rome's superiority goes to the Roman soldier's equipment and training.

Paul writes about being prepared.
Peter reminds us that we always need to be prepared to share the Gospel. We also need to be prepared to do battle with Satan.

Paul writes his letter to the Ephesians from a jail cell in Rome. He watches the Roman guards all the time and uses that strong illustration. Paul compares being prepared to the armor of a soldier, but he's talking about spiritual warfare, because we're in a spiritual battle with Satan.

☐ **THE BELT OF TRUTH** is the first part of the armor of God. For a soldier, the belt or girdle is a basic piece of equipment for strength and ease of movement. It protects his abdomen and holds his tunic in place. If his belt slips, the soldier can't move quickly and easily. In our spiritual battle everything is based on truth. The Belt of Truth is our "anchor". (How do we pursue God's truth? Do we tell the truth?)

☐ **THE BREASTPLATE OF RIGHTEOUSNESS.**
A breastplate covers the upper body, front and back, from the neck to the thighs. It protects the lungs, liver and heart. Most likely a wound to this vital area would be fatal, although a soldier could survive with injuries to his arms and legs. The most critical of all is the heart. Righteousness is our protection against evil so we have to guard our heart. (How would righteousness protect you?)

☐ **GOSPEL OF PEACE.** Proper footware is critical for a soldier. Burning hot sand, freezing snow and ice, rocks, thorns and blisters can all cause

debilitating irritation. If you can't walk, you can't fight. Two examples from history include soldiers in the American Revolution with frozen feet and those in Viet Nam jungles with fungus. We can stand strong on the Gospel of Peace. The battle has been won. Jesus Christ conquered sin and death. (Why is peace important in our relationships? How do we find peace?)

☐ **SHIELD OF FAITH.** A Roman shield looked like a door. It was often covered with leather and soaked in a flame retardant. It protected a soldier's entire body. A skillful soldier could maneuver his shield to deflect the enemy's arrows, swords and flaming darts. When soldiers joined together they could create an effective fortified defense. Faith in Jesus is our shield against Satan and temptation and it is especially powerful when Christians join together. (When has your faith in God's goodness shielded you from temptation?)

☐ **HELMET OF SALVATION.** Protection of the head is equally critical as protecting the heart. No soldier is properly equipped without a helmet. A person can go on living and fighting after the loss of a hand or foot, but cut off his head and he's out of the battle. A Roman helmet was designed to protect the head, nose and neck. Our critical battles are fought in our minds. Temptations, fear, doubt, anger and many others all begin in our thoughts. Salvation is God's promise that He will always give us the power to defeat sin. When we rely on God our mind is safe. (How can we know salvation? How can we keep our minds pure and confident?)

☐ **SWORD OF THE SPIRIT.** The first five pieces of armor are defensive; the last one is our only offensive weapon. We have to do more than just stand and defend ourselves. We have to be prepared to attack sin. The Roman sword was incredibly sharp and it cut in both directions. Jesus faced the same battles against Satan that we do. He used the Sword of the Spirit to defeat Satan. The Bible says that God's Word is the Sword of the Spirit. Only God's Word has the power to cut Satan down; we can't defeat him in our human strength. (When you are faced with temptation, what Bible verses do you say to yourself? What did Jesus use?)

We may not meet Satan face to face as Jesus did, but our battles are just as real. We need every piece of armor to stand and fight and win.

Encourage students to mentally "put on" each piece of armor every morning to help them fight the day's battles.

MEMORY VERSE

Remember this: Whoever sows sparingly will also reap sparingly, and whoever sows generously will also reap generously.

Do not be deceived: God cannot be mocked. A man reaps what he sows. Let us not become weary in doing good, for at the proper time we will reap a harvest if we do not give up.

II Corinthians 9:6
and Galatians 6:7,9
(NIV)

Story of the Sand Dollar

Upon this odd shaped sea shell
   a story grand is told
About the life of Jesus
   the wondrous tale of old.
The center marking plainly shows
   the well known Guiding Star
That led to tiny Bethlehem
   the Wise Men from afar.
The Christmas flower, Poinsettia,
   for His Nativity
The Resurrection too is marked —
   the Easter Lily, see.
Five wounds where suffered by our Lord
   from nails and Roman's spear
When He died for us on the cross
   the wounds show plainly here.
Within the shell, should it be broke
   five Doves of Peace are found
To emphasize this message so may
   Peace and Love abound.

Unknown

TREAT:

Dollar bill cookies or chocolate gold coins. Make the cookies by tinting cookie dough green and cutting into dollar size rectangles. The treat and souvenir are reminders that our real hope is in God, not money.

SOUVENIR:
SAND DOLLAR

Sea shells fit right into the cruise theme. Sand dollars are relatively easy to find from suppliers that carry seashells. You may also wish to photocopy the "Story of the Sand Dollar" and include it with the shell.

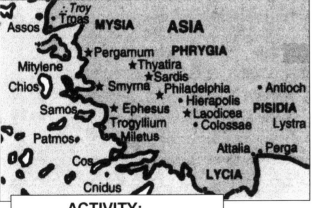

AREA INFORMATION:

The city of Ephesus was known as the temple keeper for Artemis. The temple was located outside the city and was one of the 7 wonders of the ancient world. It was 361' long and 180' wide, four times larger than the Parthenon in Athens. Ephesus was an important trading center at the junction of Asiatic caravans to the East and the sea route to Rome to the West. The main street known as the Arkadiane was made out of marble and led from the harbor to the great theatre which held 24,000 people. Ephesus was home to the Guild of Silversmiths.

ACTIVITY:

Continue taking students' photos in the armor and reviewing the meaning of each piece of armor.

LANGUAGE GREEK
This week's word to translate

Χριστος

Christos
Pronounced *"Krees-tos",* it means "anointed one."

SPECIAL EVENT:
POOL PARTY
You may want to plan another pool party. This time you could expand it to a Water Olympics theme, with different events for awards. Be sure to include lots of non-swimming water events. Remember to collect permission slips and have several adult swimmers in attendance for safety.

ACTIVITY:
BINGO
No cruise is complete without a lively game of bingo. Of course your game will be just for fun without the gambling emphasis. Use a purchased bingo game, design your own (using significant words from the lessons) or use one of the Bible bingo games available. Trophies, prizes, or Med Money can be awarded.

B	I	N	G	O
1	12	21	33	40
5	13	24	35	42
6	16	27	36	45
8	17	28	38	47
9	19	29	39	48

A lot happens to Paul in Ephesus. Many come to faith in Christ after they hear Paul preach and many others try to destroy him.

Ephesus was a cosmopolitan city and an important trade center on the west coast of Asia Minor (Turkey) on the Agean Sea. It was filled with impressive architecture including an impressive library. Because of the diversity of the city, there is great variety in the reaction of citizens to Paul's summons by the City Council. Presenting this episode as a T.V. news broadcast can help illustrate the changes and reaction of the crowd and officials.

Read through the script several times to become familiar with the action. Make extra copies of the script. Assign the speaking parts to good readers with strong voices. The rest of the class can be the audience and may express verbal reaction to the interviews. Be as creative as possible and set up a "stage" area to resemble a T.V. news studio. Use desks, chairs, microphones and scripts as well as other items you may think of. On-site reporters will need portable microphones. You can use toy or real microphones, or make some by gluing a styrofoam ball to an ice cream cone and spraying it with black paint.

- -

T.V. Broadcast based on Acts 19
"PAUL IN EPHESUS"
(Written by Linda Greenlund)

ANCHOR: Tonight we have a special report on what has been happening in the city of Ephesus. Ephesus is the most important city in the Roman province of Asia. The city is an important seaport, built around the mouth of a river. But the city of Ephesus is most famous for its temple of Artemis of Ephesus. Each year thousands of visitors flock to Ephesus to visit the temple, which is said to be one of the Seven Wonders of the ancient world. For more on this story we go to our reporter on Ephesus.

REPORTER 1: The people of Ephesus are very proud of the temple of Artemis of Ephesus. Legend has it that the statue of Artemis of Ephesus fell from the sky and landed in the city. Most of the people living in Ephesus earn their living from selling souvenirs, food, or lodging to the tourists. Artemis of Ephesus is different than the goddess Artemis in Greek myths. Artemis of Ephesus is a goddess of fertility and is very ugly in appearance. Certain events have happened recently that have rocked the city of Ephesus. Another reporter has more on this.

REPORTER 2: A man named Paul, a preacher, visited Ephesus recently and began teaching about the one true God. He stayed here for about two years and several unusual things happened while he was here. We have heard reports that handkerchiefs and aprons that Paul had handled were given to people who were sick and the people were healed. There has also been a report that some people who had practiced magic began to believe in the God of Paul and they burned their magic books. The total value of these books was 50,000 pieces of silver! Our financial expert has more on the story of the effect of Paul's preaching on the economy of Ephesus.

EXPERT: Every day people from all over Asia Minor visit the city and most buy silver statues of Artemis or temple souvenirs made by silversmiths. This spring has been the silversmiths' worst year. The whole economy has gone downhill and the preacher Paul is the cause of it. People have been listening to Paul talk about a living God who loves all people. He has told them that this God has made a way for people to know Him and that they should not worship gods made by human hands. The more Paul preaches, the fewer statues the silversmiths can sell. Rumor has it that the silversmiths are going to do something about it.

ANCHOR: We have a report that the silversmiths are meeting right now. We'll go live to that meeting.

REPORTER 3: Thank you. We're live at Demetrius's home. He has called the other silversmiths and other souvenir tradesmen together to discuss the situation with Paul. Let's listen in.

DEMETRIUS: Tradesmen of Ephesus, we have made a good living from our statues of Artemis but Paul has caused many people to turn away from our temple in Ephesus and throughout most of Asia as well. Not only are we losing money because of this man, but the temple of our great goddess Artemis is in danger. The temple might be destroyed if people stop believing in our gods.

CROWD: Great is Artemis of Ephesus! Great is Artemis of Ephesus! Great is Artemis of Ephesus!

REPORTER 3: Demetrius has certainly made the tradesmen angry with this speech. They agree with him and are ready to do something about it!

CROWD: Great is Artemis of Ephesus! Great is Artemis of Ephesus! Great is Artemis of Ephesus!

REPORTER 3: The crowd is wild and out of control. They are marching through the streets and more people are joining in the chant.

CROWD: Great is Artemis of Ephesus! Great is Artemis of Ephesus! Great is Artemis of Ephesus!

REPORTER 3: Thousands of people are marching and chanting to defend their goddess. They have rushed toward the huge outdoor amphitheater. This angry mob has nearly filled this stadium that can hold 24,000 people. They are shouting and it appears that the mob has two of Paul's followers. We go to another reporter who is closer to the action.

REPORTER 4: The two men taken captive by the crowd are indeed followers of Paul! Our sources tell us their names are Gaius and Aristarchus. This is a very serious situation. It's hard to tell what this wild crowd will do to these men. We are getting a special report from outside the amphitheater. We'll go there now.

REPORTER 5: Yes, I'm standing here with Paul, the man who has caused all this commotion. He is in hiding at the moment. Paul, what do you have to say for yourself?

PAUL: The reason I am not in the amphitheater now is that my fellow believers will not allow me to go speak to the crowd. I am not afraid to go, but my friends refuse to let me leave this place.

REPORTER 5: Isn't it true that even some of the city officials have begged you not to go near the crowd?

PAUL: Yes, it is true.

REPORTER 5: So you can see, Paul's friends and city officials have forbidden him to go to the amphitheater. With the state of the mob, it is likely that Paul would be killed if he did try to speak to the people. We'll go back to the amphitheater and see what is happening there.

CROWD: Great is Artemis of Ephesus! Great is Artemis of Ephesus! Great is Artemis of Ephesus!

REPORTER 4: As you can hear, this crowd is still angry. But some of the people don't really know what this is all about. They have followed Demetrius and his men. So there is a lot of confusion here. Pardon me, can you tell me why you are here?

MAN: I came to protest these people who say Artemis isn't a real god.

WOMAN 1: I heard everyone shouting in the streets and I came to see what all the noise was about.

WOMAN 2: I thought this was a rally for Artemis and part of the annual celebration.

REPORTER 4: Something is happening. A man is trying to get the crowd's attention so he can speak. I don't think he'll have much luck. Let's see if we can find out who he is and what he has to say.

ALEXANDER: My name is Alexander and I am a Jew. I'm trying to let the crowd know that the Jews who live in this city are not to blame for all this commotion. Paul is not one of us.

REPORTER: It doesn't look like the crowd is going to let you speak to them.

CROWD: Great is Artemis of Ephesus! Great is Artemis of Ephesus! Great is Artemis of Ephesus!

REPORTER 4: The city clerk has arrived at last. He had a hard time getting through this crowd but he is making his way to the front. The crowd is beginning to quiet down. It looks like the clerk is going to make a statement.

CLERK: Citizens of Ephesus, who in the world does not know that the city of Ephesus is the guardian of the temple and of the great goddess Artemis? We have faithfully protected the image which fell down from Zeus. Since this is true, there is no need for you to behave in this manner. These men have not robbed the temple; they have said nothing evil about our goddess. If Demetrius and his men have a legal cause against anyone, they should go to the courts and bring charges. Things must be done according to our laws! There is no reason for this disorderly gathering. The Roman government will think this is a rebellion against them if they hear about this riot. All of you go home quietly!

REPORTER 4: At last, reason has returned. The people realize that this incident has only caused more trouble for their city. Tourists may be afraid to come to Ephesus if they hear about the riot. It will make their economy even worse if that happens. As the city clerk said, if Rome hears that there was a demonstration, they will automatically think it was protesting Roman rule and they may send soldiers to take over the city. People have left and things appear to be calm for the moment.

ANCHOR: In the weeks that follow we will have to see what happens to Ephesus and to this preacher, Paul. We've heard that he left town and is heading for Macedonia. Trouble seems to follow this man. We'll keep you informed as events develop. Thank you, and good night.

Encourage students to read the biblical account, "Get the whole exciting, dramatic story for yourself. Read Acts 19."

MACEDONIA

MEMORY VERSE
Final week for
II Corinthians 9:6 and
Galatians 6:7,9

SPECIAL:
Use this week as a second opportunity for Sun-Up Breakfast.   See page 13.

TREAT
Fish shaped crackers or cookies. The sign of the fish was an early Christian symbol.

CRAFT: MUGS
Mugs are popular travel souvenirs. Purchase inexpensive plastic mugs and let students decorate them with permanent markers using a tropical or Biblical theme.

Αγαπε
Agape
Pronounced *"a-ga-pay,"* it means "unconditional love."

ACTIVITY: Pictures
Continue the Armor pictures. This is a good week to invite a missionary to your class.

LESSON 8
Theme: Love
Goal: To know that nothing can separate us from God's love and that we can show His love by encouraging others.
Bible: Acts 20

Use drama and sound effects to tell this lesson. Prepare signs and props ahead of time. Write phrases on poster board about 9"x12". #1- Yeah! #2- Please, Please, Please. #3- Tick-tock, tick-tock. #4- Oh, NO! #5- Happy Birthday to you. (#6 hold up a scroll) #7- Boo-Hoo. #8- Amen.

Choose two students who will follow directions. Give them a copy of the lesson and instruct them that they are to hold up the appropriate sign every time you reach that place in the lesson. Tell class they are to respond to the signs. When they see #1 Yeah! they are to yell Yeah! and throw confetti. Pass out confetti (#1) and tissue (#7) ahead of time. Only helpers will blow horns (#1). Helpers will hold phrases or scrolls (#6) until needed.

Based on Acts 20. Begin to read lesson: Paul had planned to leave Macedonia and meet Luke in Troas, but because of plots against him, he traveled back through Macedonia encouraging the believers. Finally it was safe for him to travel to Troas where he received a great welcome. (#1) They had waited so long for him and they didn't want him to leave. One night as he was preparing to sail for Ephesus the people in Troas begged him (#2) to teach them just a little more about Jesus.

They met on the third floor of a large house and Paul spoke for hours. About midnight (#3) a boy named

AREA INFORMATION:
Several civil wars had taken place years before Paul's visit and the poverty and hardship which resulted lasted a long time. In addition, when Rome captured the area and made it part of the Roman Empire, it took over the mines, eliminating an important source of income for the Macedonians. The Macedonians were very poor. Ancient and modern Macedonia are not the same place.

Eutychus dozed off and fell out of an open window. Luke (a doctor) confirmed that he was dead (#4). Paul rushed to him and God used Paul to raise Eutychus back to life (#1).

Everyone was amazed and excited and praising God as they returned to the house where Paul continued to teach until dawn (#3).

Paul was in a hurry to arrive in Jerusalem by Pentecost, the birthday of the church, (#5), so after leaving Troas he passed by Ephesus and traveled directly to Miletus. He sent word (#6) to the church leaders in Ephesus to meet him there. They were all excited (#1) to see each other; and Paul made one of his best speeches.

When he told them of his plans to go to Jerusalem they were upset (#4). They knew the authorities there hated him and would probably put him in prison. Paul confirmed that the Holy Spirit had warned him that trouble awaited in Jerusalem; he would never see any of them again (#7). He warned them that their future was also dangerous and he encouraged the church leaders to stay faithful and remember that nothing could separate them from God's love (#1).

As Paul headed back to the ship everyone was crying (#7), they prayed together and Paul was off to Jerusalem (#8).

Discuss lesson: Before Paul left Macedonia and Asia Minor, he traveled around encouraging his friends in the new churches. Why was that important? Be sure to invite your missionary guest to share how important encouragement is to missionaries.
What are some ways you need encouragement?
What are some ways you give encouragement?
Why is it important to remember that nothing can separate us from God's love?
Who can you encourage this week?
How can you encourage someone this week?

Port of Call #9

JERUSALEM

JOURNEY III

MEMORY VERSE

Rejoice in the Lord always. I will say it again: Rejoice! Let your gentleness be evident to all. The Lord is near. Do not be anxious about anything, but in everything, by prayer and petition, with thanksgiving, present your requests to God. And the peace of God, which transcends all understanding, will guard your hearts and your minds in Christ Jesus.

I can do everything through him who gives me strength.

Philippians 4:4-7, 13

ACTIVITY-TREAT:

Use this lesson as an opportunity to meet somewhere other than your usual class room. If possible, find a grassy area outdoors. Spread out blankets to sit on and set up a folding table to prepare and serve a snack. Cooking fish sticks on an outdoor grill adds a fun atmosphere. Be sure to start the fire early enough so that the fish sticks will cook thoroughly over coals. Assign an adult to watch the fire at all times; have sand and water available to extinguish the fire. Pour juice in advance, serve fish shaped crackers in a basket and have ketchup available for students who want it. Plan to cook fish sticks about 10 minutes on each side during the lesson, and serve after lesson.

CRAFT-SOUVENIR:
Fish Magnet

The fish symbol reflects the cruise theme as well as the early Christian symbol ΙΧΘΥΣ (*ik-thuse* means fish).

Shop for a piece of fabric with a colorful fish pattern or buy a piece of colorful fabric and cut out fish shapes. Using white glue or fusible web attach fish to poster board. Have students cut out the fish, glue a small magnet on the back and decorate the front with fabric paint and glitter.

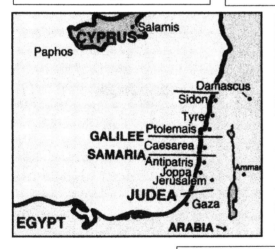

AREA INFORMATION:

Situated high above the surrounding territory, there are several hills within the walls of Jerusalem including Mt. Zion and the Temple Mount. Jerusalem is less than 11 acres, built on terraces. It has been destroyed and rebuilt many times. Conquered and occupied by various invading armies, it was a walled city when it was captured by David to be his capital. It was the most important of Solomon's royal cities because of the temple. The city grew under King Herod to a population of about 200,000. Herod was a builder. He rebuilt the temple, a palace, an amphitheatre, theatre and a fort. Jerusalem is also known as the City of God, Zion, and the Holy City. Loosely translated, Jerusalem means "City of Peace."

LANGUAGE: GREEK
This week's word is

ΙΧΘΥΣ

ICHTHUS
Pronounced *"ik-thuse"*, it literally means "fish." It was an early Christian symbol, an acrostic for Jesus Christ God's Son Savior

SPECIAL: MEDDIE HUNT

Incorporate a short hunt for Meddie into this "out of the classroom" session. A note could be found in the room instructing you to meet MC at a designated place (where you'll have the cook-out). The note could say that MC is sure he has Meddie trapped and he needs help to rescue the treasure.

Upon arrival, students will find a glowing camp fire and fish sticks on the grill. Of course they'll also find another note: *"Well, Meddie slipped out of the trap, but I'm hot on her trail. Look around and see if she left the treasure behind. And, enjoy the cook-out. See you soon."* MC If you choose to hide a treasure chest, there could be a note inside it too, from Meddie: *"This chest was too heavy so I just took the treasure and headed to...."*

LESSON 9 JERUSALEM

THEME: Wisdom

GOAL: Discuss how to put our confidence in God's wisdom and the knowledge that nothing can separate us from His love.

BIBLE: Acts 21, 22

This Port of Call is Jerusalem (stamp passports for Jerusalem), but the events actually begin in Tyre, then move to Caesarea before finally arriving in Jerusalem. Be sure to read Acts 21 and 22 several times to become familiar with all the action and be able to retell it with a few notes. This is a good visual lesson, so plan to use props as you recount this final part of Paul's Third Journey.

You'll need an old suitcase or sport bag to conceal the props until the proper time. If it shows some sign of wear and tear that will add to the visual effect. You'll also need: a toy turkey, a toy tire, birthday candles, a belt, a heart, a dove, a scroll, a tile with "G-E-N" printed on it (to represent Gentiles), a Band Aid®, a piece of chain, a Star of David, and a whip. If you're unable to locate actual or plastic items, pictures or drawings will also work. If you want dessert for your snack you may want to use an actual birthday cake instead of just the candles. When you've gathered all of your props, pack them in your suit case.

Begin the lesson by reviewing last week and adding a few details about Paul concluding his Third Missionary Journey to Asia Minor (Turkey) and Europe and heading back to Jerusalem.

Paul left Macedonia and Asia Minor knowing that he would never see his friends there again. There were a lot of sad good byes, but all the time Paul was encouraging the people he visited. He kept reminding them that nothing can separate us from God's love.

As you use the symbols to tell the lesson you may want to read or paraphrase the Scripture passage or have a student read it.

Next, pull the **turkey** out of the bag and tell how Paul and Luke were saying good-bye to the churches as they sailed south down the coast of Turkey (Acts 21:1-3). Show the **tire** as you tell that the ship docked in Tyre and Paul found a group of Christians who begged him not to go to Jerusalem (Acts 21:3-6). Reveal the **birthday candles (or cake)** as you tell how Paul was determined to be in Jerusalem to celebrate Pentecost (see note at end of page) so he said his farewells and headed to Caesarea (Acts 21:7-8).

In Caesarea, a believer named Agabus predicted Paul's fate. Hold up the **belt**, (Acts 21:9-11). Next, hold up the **heart**. The church in Caesarea told Paul

they loved him and begged him not to go to Jerusalem. But Paul was determined and told them he was ready to die for Jesus (Acts 21:12-14). The dove represents believers. Show the **dove**. Believers from Caesarea accompanied Paul to Jerusalem (Acts 21:15-19).

Pull the **scroll** out of your bag. Church leaders became very concerned because there were rumors in Jerusalem that Paul was disregarding Moses and the Law (Acts 21:20-26). Some Jews at the temple in Jerusalem were telling lies. Hold up the **GEN-tile symbol**. They said Paul had let Gentiles into the Temple (Acts 21:27-29). Show the **Band Aid®**. They dragged Paul out and beat him until Roman officials broke it up (Acts 21:30-32). Hold up the **chain**. After rescuing Paul from the mob, the Romans locked him up in chains in Antonio Fortress (Acts 21:33-36).

Paul spoke Greek to the Romans, but he used Hebrew to speak to the Jews. Show the **Star of David.** He defended himself and argued he would never take a Gentile into the temple. He detailed his Jewish heritage and told about his conversion on the road to Damascus. But when he spoke about taking the Gospel to the Gentiles because the Jews refused the Good News, a riot broke out (Acts 21:37-22:21).

Show the **whip**. The Romans were quick to break up the riot and the Commander ordered Paul whipped. At this point Paul revealed that he was a Roman citizen! (Acts 22:22-29) (Do not uncoil the whip.)

Use the props to quiz students about events in the lesson during the snack time.

(TURKEY) Asia Minor is now called? *(Turkey)*
Paul sailed back to Israel from? (Turkey)

(TIRE) Paul's ship landed at the city of? *(Tyre)*

(CANDLES) Paul wanted to be in Jerusalem to celebrate? *(Pentecost)*

(BELT) Agabus predicted that Paul would? *(Be bound and taken prisoner)*

(HEART) Paul's friends loved him and begged him? *(Not to go to Jerusalem)*

(DOVE) Believers from *(Caesarea)* accompanied Paul to? *(Jerusalem)*

(SCROLL) Paul honored *(the Jewish Law)*

("GEN" TILE) There was trouble at? *(the Temple because people lied about Paul taking Gentiles in)*

(BAND AID®) *(the crowd beat Paul)*

(CHAIN) The authorities rescued Paul and *(took him off to jail)*

(STAR OF DAVID) Paul preached to the Jews in *(Hebrew)*

Note: Pentecost, also known as Shovous, is the 4th Feast Day in Leviticus, (Leviticus 23:15-22) After Jesus went back to heaven, the disciples were in Jerusalem celebrating Pentecost when the Holy Spirit came to them, (Acts 2:1-4). Today Christians celebrate Pentecost as the birthday of the Church.

MEMORY VERSE

Rejoice in the Lord always. I will say it again: Rejoice! Let your gentleness be evident to all. The Lord is near. Do not be anxious about anything, but in everything, by prayer and petition, with thanksgiving, present your requests to God. And the peace of God, which transcends all understanding, will guard your hearts and your minds in Christ Jesus.

I can do everything through him who gives me strength.

Philippians 4:4-7, 13
(NIV)

ACTIVITY: QUOITS

Quoits is another deck game popular on cruise ships. You'll need six hoops 6-8 inches in diameter made from heavy rope. (Or use plastic lids.) Mark three with colored tape. Now draw three concentric circles on the floor or parking lot with chalk; the smallest circle about 12″ across and the largest about 3′ across. Assign value to each section: 5 - 10 - 15 points. Divide class into teams. Each team gets three hoops. Teams alternate tossing the hoops onto the target. Each team member has three tosses and can try to knock the other teams' hoops off of the target. Total scores after everyone has had a turn and award prizes or Med Money.

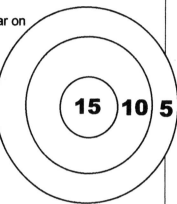

AREA INFORMATION:

The city of Caesarea is located on one of the three international north/south roads running through Israel. The Red Sea Road also known as King's Highway ran from Damascus to the Gulf of Aqabah. King Herod built Caesarea on the Roman pattern with an amphitheater, market, harbor, temple to Augustus, fountains, good streets and houses. Herod created an artificial harbor for the city. An aqueduct carried water over five miles from springs on the south slopes of Mt. Carmel. Roman procurators were based in Caesarea. They included Pontius Pilate AD26-36, Felix AD52-60 and Festus AD60-62.

Sidon
Tyre
Ptolemais
GALILEE
Caesarea
SAMARIA
Antipatris
Joppa
Jerusalem
JUDEA
Gaza
ARABIA ⤵

CRAFT: Water Bottle & Carrier

This week's craft, souvenir and treat are combined. Purchase individual size, filled, plastic drinking water bottles. Be sure the bottles have a neck area and a "lip" below the cap. Students measure rope or macramé cord to make a shoulder strap (about 40″). Loop around neck of bottle and tie a secure knot. Tie off ends with an overhand knot. Water bottle can be carried over your shoulder leaving your hands free.

LANGUAGE: GREEK

This week's words to translate

βιβλος
biblos
Pronounced "*bee-bloss*", it means "book." The word "Bible" comes from biblos.

λογος
logos
Pronounced "*low-goss*", it means "the word." See John 1:1.

LESSON 10 CAESAREA

THEME: Faith

GOAL: To know that our faith in God will give us the strength to face opposition

BIBLE: Acts 22:30-Acts 26

After the incident at the temple in Jerusalem and near riot, Paul finds himself on trial in Caesarea. Read over the events beginning in Acts 22:30. Then divide the class and stage your own trial. First choose a judge and jury and divide the rest of the class into the defense and prosecution. Each side needs to choose a lawyer. Allow 10-20 minutes for each side to prepare their case. (Or, send instructions home with students the week before and ask them to arrive prepared.) All witness testimony and arguments must come from the Bible. There is enough information in the previous lessons for both the defense and prosecution. If possible, invite a lawyer to participate in this class. There are many possible witnesses for the defense. Here are a few suggestions to get you started.

The Prosecution accuses Paul, and presents its witnesses first:

■ **Prosecutor:** "I accuse Paul of violating the temple and trying to start a riot."

■ From Ephesus: "Paul is definitely responsible for the riot. The silversmiths couldn't just stand by as he told people to destroy their idols and occult books. The silversmiths and sorcerers would be out of business. I have proof — ashes from an actual burned occult book." Acts 19:19

■ From Galatia: "After performing several tricks to fool the people, Paul and Barnabas suddenly left Iconium." Acts 14:6

■ From Philippi: "So why was he in jail in the first place? We don't put innocent people in jail. We've always been suspicious that the earthquake may not have been truly an act of nature." Acts 17:22

■ From Corinth: "I personally heard Paul tell men that they were temples of God." I Corinthians 3:16-17

■ From Jerusalem: "Well, I was in Jerusalem and Paul definitely took Gentiles into the temple." Acts 21:27-28

Possible closing arguments for the prosecution:

■ "You must find Paul guilty. With his history of stirring up trouble in Laodocia, Philippi, Thessalonica, Ephesus and numerous Roman cities, no doubt that he deliberately staged a demonstration at the temple to disrupt the city during the holiday.

Now the Defense defends Paul and presents its witnesses:

✠ From Philippi, after the earthquake: "Paul could have saved his own life, instead he made all the prisoners stay in their cells and he didn't try to escape himself. He saved many lives." Acts 16:26-30

✠ From Troas, "Paul was so concerned, he stopped preaching and rushed to Eutychus who had fallen 3 stories to his death. Paul raised him back to life!" Acts 20:7-11

✠ From Corinth: "Paul challenged us to give an offering for the poor in Jerusalem and he took it to them." I Corinthians 16:1-3

✠ From Ephesus: "The silversmiths started the riot, not Paul." Acts 19:17-41

✠ From Jerusalem: "Paul fasted, prayed and purified himself as our law requires. I went to the temple with Paul. We were all Jews." Acts 21:17-26

✠ From Thessalonica: "The Jews themselves actually stirred up the people and started the riots in Antioch, Thessalonica, Ephesus and other cities, not Paul." Acts 13:50, 14:2,19; 16:22, 17:13

✠ Last witness, the Apostle Paul. "My accusers cannot prove the charge that I stirred up trouble. I am a follower of Jesus and worship the God of our fathers. I believe in the Law and the prophets and want a clear conscience. I believe in the same God as my accusers. They charged me with no crime before the Sanhedrin except the belief in the resurrection of Jesus. This whole trial is because of the resurrection." Acts 23:6-14

After testimony there could be motions to dismiss by the defense:

◎ Dismiss all charges because they're based on lies and assumptions, not fact.

◎ Dismiss the case because witnesses under oath are deliberately giving false testimony.

◎ Dismiss the case because the real charges are religious, not civil and Rome shouldn't be involved.

Conduct the class as much like a real trial as possible. Encourage the "lawyers" to object to testimony and have the judge rule on them. After all the testimony is finished, have the jury discuss the charges in private and then read the verdict to the class. Read portions of Paul's real trial from the Bible and summarize the situation. Acts 23-26

This trial led to Paul's fourth journey to Rome and prison.

MEMORY VERSE

Rejoice in the Lord always. I will say it again: Rejoice! Let your gentleness be evident to all. The Lord is near. Do not be anxious about anything, but in everything, by prayer and petition, with thanksgiving, present your requests to God. And the peace of God, which transcends all understanding, will guard your hearts and your minds in Christ Jesus.

I can do everything through him who gives me strength.

Philippians 4:4-7, 13
NIV

ACTIVITY:
Create A Storm

Divide class into four groups. The first group will snap their fingers to sound like rain drops. The second group will blow, hum and howl to sound like the wind. Group three will slap their hands on their thighs to sound like heavy rain and the fourth group will stomp their feet to sound like thunder.

Begin slowly and softly with gentle rain drops. Add a little wind. Gradually add heavy rain and increase the wind. Finally add thunder to create a raging storm. Then the storm begins to die down. Fade out the thunder. Slow down the heavy rain and wind. Stop the heavy rain. Stop the wind. Continue soft rain and gradually stop. The storm is over.

TREAT:
Gummy snakes (candy) sold packaged and in bulk in most grocery stores to remind us of Paul's courage in time of danger.

PROJECT:

Have students make invitations for their parents for the Evening Cruise Buffet next week.

AREA INFORMATION:

Malta is a tiny island in the Mediterranean Sea, about 60 miles south of Sicily. The word "Malta" means refuge. It is strategically located between several ancient and modern nations competing for control of the Mediterranean region.

LANGUAGE:
GREEK

αγγελος
aggelos

Pronounced "*a-gay-loss*," it means "angel" or "messenger."

CRAFT: Visor

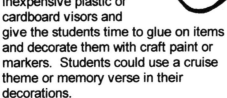

This week's craft and souvenir are combined. Purchase inexpensive plastic or cardboard visors and give the students time to glue on items and decorate them with craft paint or markers. Students could use a cruise theme or memory verse in their decorations.

SPECIAL:
Final Meddie skit. MC drops in to say that he's pretty sure Meddie is on her way to a small island off the coast of Italy, and he has to get going before the trail gets cold. He leaves his internet number so he can be reached with further Meddie information.

LESSON 11

MALTA

THEME: Courage

GOAL: We can show courage in facing difficult situations because we can pray and trust God to provide us with courage and peace.

BIBLE: Acts 27-28:10

After Paul's trial before King Agrippa and Festus in Caesarea, it was decided that his trial should be continued in Rome. Actually Agrippa would have dismissed the charges, but Paul was a Roman citizen and he had appealed to Rome, so he was put on board a prison ship headed for Italy. Paul's fourth journey was a prison journey.

This is a great lesson to act out, because it is full of drama and excitement.

Prepare for this lesson by gathering some props. You'll need:
  a blue blanket or sheet
  large and small cardboard boxes
  construction paper
  string
  pillow cases stuffed with crumpled
  newspaper
  anchor
  a sword for the Roman guard
  twigs
  rubber snake.

Use large cardboard boxes to design a "boat" on the floor.
Use smaller boxes for cargo; tie with string.
Cut an anchor from construction paper and attach a string.
Tie the pillow cases closed with string.

Begin by spreading the blue blanket on the floor to represent the water of the Mediterranean Sea. Place the" boat" in the center of the "water".
Load the boat with boxes and bags for cargo.
Put the anchor and sword on board.

Leave the twigs and snake off to one side.

Now choose students to act as crew, Roman guards, passengers, and the Apostle Paul.

Tell them to listen carefully as you read the lesson from the Bible and to act out the action as you read. Encourage them to be very dramatic. Tell them to get on board.

Seat the remainder of the class in a circle around the boat. They will provide the sound effects for the storm in Acts 27:18-20. (See Activity directions on page 33.)

Acts 27:6-28:20
Read slowly and dramatically. Encourage students in the boat if they don't respond spontaneously.

Begin the storm at verse 18 and calm it down after verse 20.

After the drama, remind the class that God had promised Paul that no one would die even though the ship and cargo were all lost.

DISCUSSION QUESTIONS

Have students discuss what is the most valuable thing to have and to save in the midst of a terrible disaster (like an earthquake, flood, or fire). Maybe a student will have a firsthand experience to share.

The second part of the discussion should be about accepting honor that is not rightly ours.
• How do you think Paul felt when the people on Malta wanted to worship him?
• What can happen when we accept honor we don't deserve?

THINK ABOUT IT - TALK ABOUT IT

How has God used a disaster in your life as an opportunity?

What stops you from getting involved in the lives of others?

Who are some people who have been involved in your life? In what way?

If your life were a chapter in the Book of Acts, what would it be about?

✦ Hand out invitations to the Evening Buffet next week.

✦ Announce the Souvenir Shop for next week. In preparation for the Souvenir Shop, ask students how much Med Money they each have, so you can set appropriate prices allowing students to "buy" several items.

MEMORY VERSE

Rejoice in the Lord always. I will say it again: Rejoice! Let your gentleness be evident to all. The Lord is near. Do not be anxious about anything, but in everything, by prayer and petition, with thanksgiving, present your requests to God. And the peace of God, which transcends all understanding, will guard your hearts and your minds in Christ Jesus.

I can do everything through him who gives me strength.

Philippians 4:4-7, 13
(NIV)

SPECIAL: EVENING BUFFET

You can make this event as simple or as fancy as you like. Ask several parents to help you by supplying some of the refreshments. You could choose a Mediterranean menu such as pizza, spaghetti, Greek salad, and baklava. Or a general selection of salads, casseroles and desserts. Set up the room with special decorations. Maybe you will want to include a brief program and ask some of the students to share a memorable experience of the "cruise." Have photo albums

available and show the slides (if you took them). Use the evening as a special time to socialize with parents and kids.

ACTIVITY: SOUVENIR SHOP

Purchase snacks, treats and inexpensive gifts from discount stores and mail-order catalogs. Set up "shop" in your classroom. Mark prices on items. Following the lesson allow students to browse for a while and then use their Med money to purchase souvenirs and treats. Price items from $1 to $50. Be sure to ask the students the week before how much Med Money they have earned. This will help with the pricing. You'll need enough inexpensive items so each student can buy several.

AREA INFORMATION:

Rome was one of the two largest cities in the world in the first century with a population of one million. It was the political capital of the Roman Empire and often called the eternal city. Rome is a city of seven hills on the Tiber River. In the first century, it was surrounded by a wall over 13 miles in circumference. It was full of temples, theatres, forums, palaces, baths, administrative buildings, triumphal arches, colonnades, circuses (a circus was a round building), fine roads and gardens. The forum, in the heart of the city, is bounded by four of the seven hills. Ordinary people lived in tenements, three to four stories tall. Poorly built, they often collapsed or burned. There were many poor and unemployed in first century Rome and the government was required to provide them with wheat. No longer the ruler of the world, Rome today is the capital of Italy, and the center for the Roman Catholic Church. It is full of ruins and great works of art which remind us of its powerful past and significant events of the first century Church.

TREAT:
Juice and cookies.

REMINDER:

Remind students that tonight will be the evening buffet to celebrate the end of the cruise. Family and friends are invited.

ROME

THEME: Truth

GOAL: Discuss how we can choose to redeem the time (use our time wisely) to glorify God and tell the Truth of Jesus Christ.

BIBLE: Acts 28

Acts 28 concludes Paul's journeys with his arrival in Rome. Paul had hoped to appear before Caesar, plead his case, and be released. Instead he found himself under house arrest. He was allowed to find his own place to live, but he had to be chained to a Roman soldier at all times.

After a few days of waiting, Paul asked the Jewish leaders to meet with him. He explained that he had done nothing to hurt the Jews and they agreed that they had heard nothing bad about him. They wanted to hear what Paul had been teaching, and he was very happy to tell them the message of redemption through Jesus Christ. Some believed that Jesus was the Messiah and that he had died for their sins and they put their faith in him.

Paul remained a prisoner in his house in Rome for two years. Many people visited him to hear about Jesus and they were impressed that Paul wasn't depressed and complaining about his situation. Paul's circumstances did not shape his attitude. He used his time wisely, he redeemed the time, by sharing God's message of love and salvation with everyone he could. He also used the time to write letters to his friend, Philemon, and to the churches at Colosse and Ephesus.

In the King James Version, (Ephesians 5:16), Paul tells us to "redeem the time for the days are evil." Discuss with the class what it means to "redeem the time." *To use our time wisely; to tell the message of salvation in Jesus Christ; to use our words and actions to glorify God regardless of the circumstances.*

The book of Acts ends with Paul still under house arrest in Rome. Historical tradition says that Paul was released, re-arrested and executed in Rome.

This is a good time to review Paul's journeys.

Tick - Tick - Tick

Set up an object table to help jog students' memories. Items, or pictures, on the table could include: rocks, Dramamine (motion sickness medication), keys, hymnal, crystal ball, idol, matches, aspirin, passport, boat, swim fin, Greek coins, Band Aids®, snake, letter, sandal, purple cloth, umbrella, and a chain. Cover the table

Show the class one of the objects and tell what it symbolizes. Uncover the table. After students have had some time to view the table, set a stop watch for one minute and challenge students (one at a time or in small groups) to tell as much as they can in 60 seconds of how Paul redeemed the time or used disasters to tell others about Jesus. Then use some of the objects to tell the class about situations they may not recall or associate with an object.

ROCKS One city stoned Paul for preaching, but he didn't stop. He moved on to another city and preached there.

DRAMAMINE Paul *redeemed* the storm by telling everyone onboard about the storm maker, God.

KEYS An earthquake unlocked Paul's jail cell, but he stayed around to *redeem* the jailer.

HYMNAL Paul and Silas *redeemed the time* in prison by singing hymns and praying.

CRYSTAL BALL Paul *redeemed* the slave girl by casting out the evil spirit.

IDOL (statue) Paul preached the Gospel of Christ and the people destroyed their idols.

MATCHES (You may want to use an empty box.) People were *redeemed* from occultic control and burned their evil books.

ASPIRIN Paul was abused, beaten, arrested and falsely accused, but these headaches didn't stop him from *redeeming the time*.

PASSPORT Paul traveled all over the Mediterranean area with the *message of redemption*, that Christ died for their sins.

BOAT Paul spent a lot of time on the water, giving him an opportunity to preach to the crew.

SWIM FIN After the ship wreck everyone swam to shore safely.

GREEK COINS Paul spent a lot of time in Greece sharing the Gospel and starting churches.

BAND AIDS® Paul was beaten and physically abused many times just for talking about Jesus.

SNAKE (rubber) Paul refused to be called a god when he didn't die from the bite of a poisonous snake. He gave Almighty God the glory.

LETTER Paul used part of his time in prison to write letters encouraging friends and churches.

SANDAL On land Paul walked from town to town to spread the *message of redemption*.

PURPLE CLOTH Lydia,who sold purple cloth, was the first European Christian when she responded to the *message of redemption*.

UMBRELLA Paul assured everyone that God had promised that no one would die in the shipwreck.

CHAIN Paul was arrested and put in chains for teaching about Jesus so he preached the *message of redemption* to the other prisoners and the guards.

God gave Paul the mission to share the Gospel with as many people as possible and He also gave him the strength to do it. Paul didn't use his circumstances as excuses not to preach, but he used them to accomplish his mission. This is our challenge as well. How can we follow his example and redeem the time in our lives?

Idea and Resource Pages

LATE NIGHT BUFFET

Celebrate the end of the cruise with a Late Night Buffet farewell dinner for students and parents. Arrange a potluck supper. Show photos and souvenirs and talk about the different Ports.

CLASS POSTCARDS

Here's an idea for keeping in touch with your students. Create a post card for some or all of your ports of call. Send them to students who missed a particular week. Also, you could send them to the entire class in advance telling them you are looking forward to seeing them on an up coming port of call.

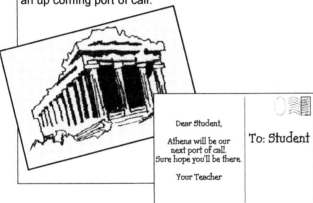

Dear Student,

Athens will be our next port of call. Sure hope you'll be there.

Your Teacher

To: Student

PORT SIGNS

Check the overview, pages 4-5, for ports and descriptions of the lifestyle and attitude of the area. Design a sign for each port. Here are some examples of how your port signs could look. Post the port signs, in order, above your map. (See p.3).

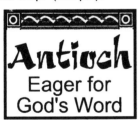

Antioch
Eager for
God's Word

Caesarea
Peaceful,
Prosperous

MILE MARKERS

Design mileage signs for your class.

Example, from Los Angeles:

Rome - 6763 miles
Athens - 7386 miles
Jerusalem - 8175 miles

SAMPLE SCRIPT IDEAS FOR MEDDIE

Note: Meddie is the Loch Med Monster, nicknamed Meddie. The idea is copied from the Loch Ness Monster nicknamed Nessie. Loch (pronounced lock) is the Scottish word for lake. Med stands for the Mediterranean Sea where Paul traveled.

On the first day of class MC (MC stands for Monster Catcher) rushes into the room at a pre-determined time. MC is mostly a monologue with the teacher making brief comments.

MC "Have you seen her? I know she came this way, I've been following her for a week! You must have seen her, she's huge, and sort of green..."

TEACHER "Excuse me, who?"

MC "Meddie of course, you know, the Loch Med Monster. Usually lives in the Mediterranean Sea," (looks around and points to map on wall.) "Right about here."

TEACHER "Well... er..."

MC "She has a treasure cave you know. And she has the nasty habit of just taking whatever she likes, and I'm sure she stashes it in her treasure cave."

TEACHER "I'm sure..."

MC walks over and picks up a candy wrapper (or your choice of some "treasure") planted earlier. "A ha! She has definitely been here. Haven't you noticed that there are fewer and fewer candy bars in the stores these days? She's a chocoholic! She's carrying it all off to her treasure cave." MC's pager goes off. "Gotta go. I'll be back when I have news. Oh, yes, keep a close eye on your candy bars."

Plan for one or two more visits from MC. He could bring a blurry photo of what he thinks is Meddie and a "wanted poster" to put up in the classroom, and/or a chocolate bar with "Meddie teeth marks".

The Meddie Hunt is described on page 29.

The final Meddie skit should be on the next to last class or the last class. MC can arrive with a really hot lead. There are confirmed reports of the over-powering smell of chocolate coming from a small island off of the southern tip of Italy. There have also been giant chocolate chip shaped clouds seen over the island. So, MC is anxious to get started and he thanks the class for being part of his adventure and bids them farewell.

SUPPLIES

☐ Oriental Trading Company has an extensive catalog of inexpensive gifts and prizes as well as some craft supplies. Call 1-800-228-2269 for a catalog. The mailing address is P.O. Box 3407, Omaha, NE 68103-0407.

☐ SAS has an illustrated catalog of craft supplies and kits. Call 1-800-243-9232 to get a catalogue.

☐ Check with a local travel agent and ask for a travel brochure or posters of Mediterranean cruises.

☐ Check with a local coin dealer for samples of money from a Mediterranean country.

☐ Check your local library for a book of international flags. You could copy the designs and use flags from different Mediterranean countries for room decorations.

☐ Check the yellow pages of your phone book for international restaurants. You might want to have a special treat such as baklava or falafel from Turkey, Israel, Greece or Italy at one class.

☐ Representatives from foreign countries usually have offices in large cities. Perhaps you could locate a consulate or visitors bureau for Israel, Greece, Italy, or Turkey and ask them to send you travel information about their country.

HEBREW ALPHABET

The Hebrew language is written from right to left. The 22 character alphabet is made up of all consonants. In modern Hebrew the vowels are indicated by "pointing." The basis for the word "alphabet" is found in the first two letters, aleph and bet. When writing students names use the aleph for an "a" sound, use the yod for a "j" and "long e" sound and use the vav for either "o" or "u". Aleph and Ayin have no sound of their own. They take their sound from the vowels near them in a word. Several letters have a final form which is used when it is the last letter in a word. Het is a guttural h as in Hanukkah.

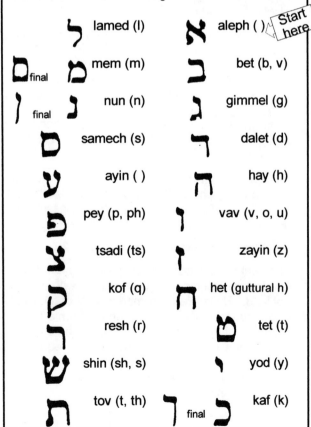

lamed (l)		aleph ( )	Start here
mem (m) final		bet (b, v)	
nun (n) final		gimmel (g)	
samech (s)		dalet (d)	
ayin ( )		hay (h)	
pey (p, ph)		vav (v, o, u)	
tsadi (ts)		zayin (z)	
kof (q)		het (guttural h)	
resh (r)		tet (t)	
shin (sh, s)		yod (y)	
tov (t, th)		kaf (k) final	

GREEK ALPHABET

Greek is written left to right, just like English. There are 24 letters in the alphabet, and Greek uses upper and lower case. Many Greek letters are similar to English, especially upper case. The English equivalent is noted in parenthesis. There is no "C" in Greek, use a Κ or Σ to get the proper sound. Use Χ (chi, pronounced key) for a hard, guttural "k" sound as in Christ. Use Ι for "J".

Αα	alpha (a)	Νν	nu (n)
Ββ	beta (b)	Ξξ	xi (x)
Γγ	gamma (g) hard	Οο	omicron (o) short
Δδ	delta (d)	Ππ	pi (p)
Εε	epsilon (e) short	Ρρ	rho (r)
Ζζ	zeta (z)	Σσ	sigma (s)
		ς	s at the end of a word
Ηη	eta (e) long	Ττ	tau (t)
Θθ	theta (th)	Υυ	upsilon (u)
Ιι	iota (i)	Φφ	Phi (f)
Κκ	kappa (k)	Χχ	chi (guttural k, similar to the Hebrew het.)
Λλ	lamda (l)	Ψψ	psi (ps)
Μμ	mu (m)	Ωω	omega (o) long

Photo copy pages 39 and 40. Trim bottom edge of page 40 and connect to page 39 by overlapping and gluing in place.

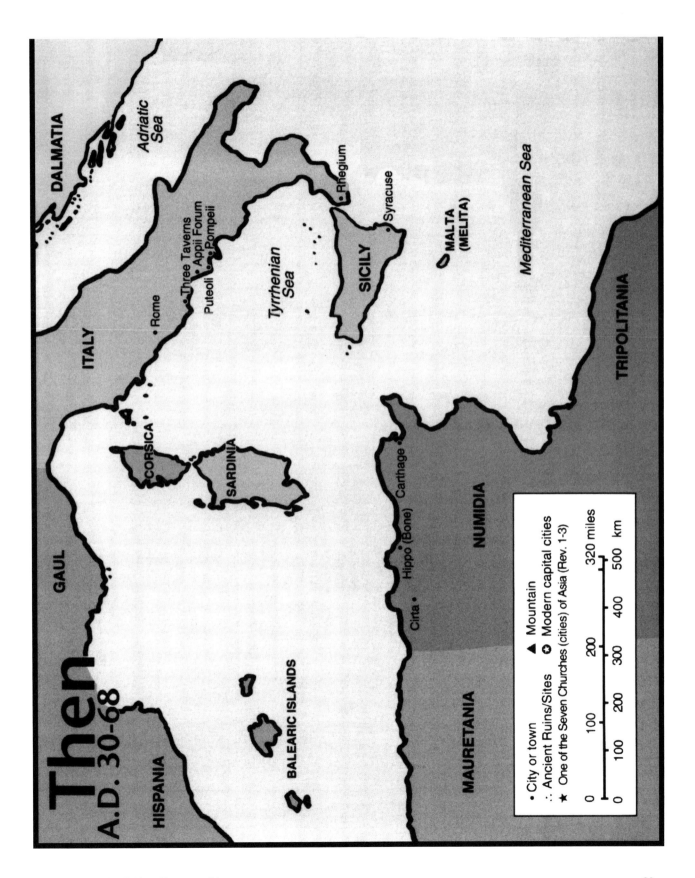

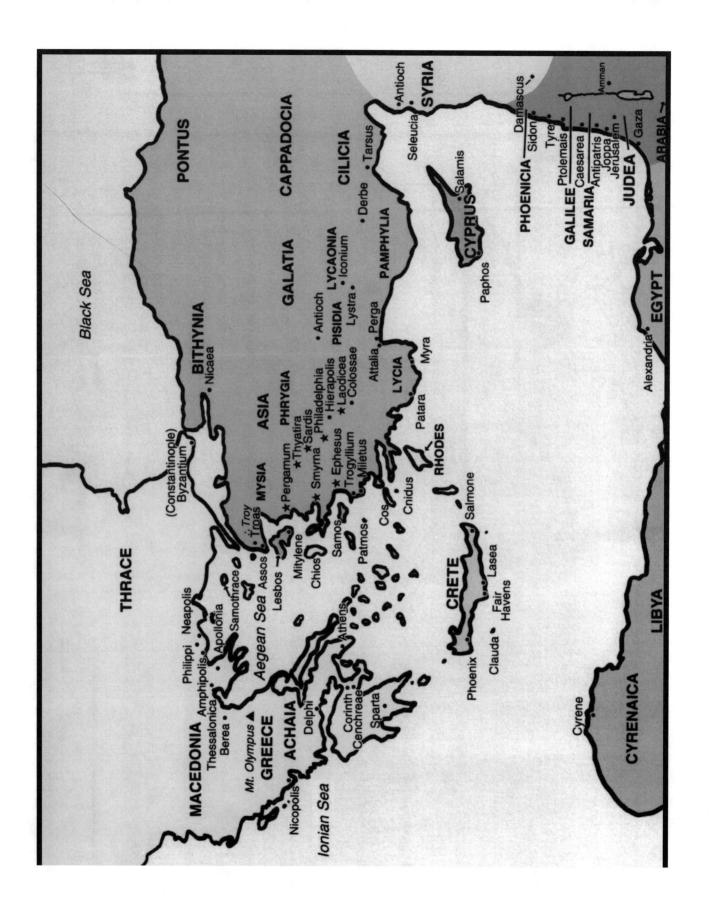

Black Sea

THRACE

PONTUS

CAPPADOCIA

BITHYNIA
Nicaea •

(Constantinople)
Byzantium

ASIA

PHRYGIA

GALATIA

LYCAONIA
Iconium •

PISIDIA
• Antioch
Lystra •
Derbe •

CILICIA
• Tarsus

SYRIA
• Antioch
Seleucia •

Damascus •

PHOENICIA
Sidon
Tyre
Ptolemais •
Caesarea •
Antipatris •
Joppa •
Jerusalem •
Gaza •

Amman •

ARABIA →

GALILEE
SAMARIA
JUDEA

CYPRUS
Salamis •

Paphos •

PAMPHYLIA
Attalia• Perga

★ Pergamum
★ Thyatira
★ Smyrna ★ Sardis
★ Philadelphia
• Hierapolis
★ Laodicea
• Colossae

MYSIA

Troy
Troas •

Ephesus ★
Trogyllium •
Miletus •

Samos •

Chios

Mitylene

Lesbos

Assos
Samothrace

Apollonia •

Patmos •

LYCIA
Patara
Myra

RHODES

Cnidus

Cos •

CRETE
Salmone

Lasea
Fair
Havens

Phoenix
Clauda •

Philippi
Neapolis
Amphipolis •
Thessalonica
Berea •

MACEDONIA

Aegean Sea

Mt. Olympus ▲

GREECE

Delphi

ACHAIA

Athens •

Corinth •
Cenchreae •

Sparta •

Nicopolis •

Ionian Sea

EGYPT

Alexandria •

LIBYA

Cyrene •

CYRENAICA